It's another great book from CGP...

There are only three ways to make sure you're fully prepared for the new Grade 9-1 GCSE Biology exams — practise, practise and practise.

That's why we've packed this brilliant CGP book with realistic exam-style questions for every topic, and we've got all the practicals covered too.

And since you'll be tested on a wide range of topics in the real exams, we've also included a section of mixed questions to keep you on your toes!

CGP — still the best! ☺

Our sole aim here at CGP is to produce the highest quality books — carefully written, immaculately presented and dangerously close to being funny.

Then we work our socks off to get them out to you — at the cheapest possible prices.

Contents

✓ Use the tick boxes to check off the topics you've completed.

Published by CGP

Editors: Ciara McGlade, Rachael Rogers, Hayley Thompson

Contributors: Bethan Parry, Alison Popperwell

With thanks to Susan Alexander, Charlotte Burrows, Katherine Faudemer and Sarah Pattison for the proofreading.

ISBN: 978 1 78294 495 9

Percentile growth chart on page 18 copyright © 2009 Royal College of Paediatrics and Child Health.

Page 37 contains public sector information licensed under the Open Government Licence v 3.0.
http://www.nationalarchives.gov.uk/doc/open-government-licence/version/3/

Definition of health in answers to p53: Preamble to the Constitution of the World Health Organization as adopted by the International Health Conference, New York, 19 June - 22 July 1946; signed on 22 July 1946 by the representatives of 61 States (Official Records of the World Health Organization, no. 2, p. 100) and entered into force on 7 April 1948.

All references to Warfarin throughout the book are Warfarin™.

Every effort has been made to locate copyright holders and obtain permission to reproduce sources. For those sources where it has been difficult to trace the originator of the work, we would be grateful for information. If any copyright holder would like us to make an amendment to the acknowledgements, please notify us and we will gladly update the book at the next reprint. Thank you.

Clipart from Corel®
Printed by Elanders Ltd, Newcastle upon Tyne

Based on the classic CGP style created by Richard Parsons.

How to Use This Book

- Hold the book <u>upright</u>, approximately <u>50 cm</u> from your face, ensuring that the text looks like <u>this</u>, not <u>sᴉɥʇ</u>. Alternatively, place the book on a <u>horizontal</u> surface (e.g. a table or desk) and sit adjacent to the book, at a distance which doesn't make the text too small to read.

- In case of emergency, press the two halves of the book together <u>firmly</u> in order to close.

- Before attempting to use this book, familiarise yourself with the following <u>safety information</u>:

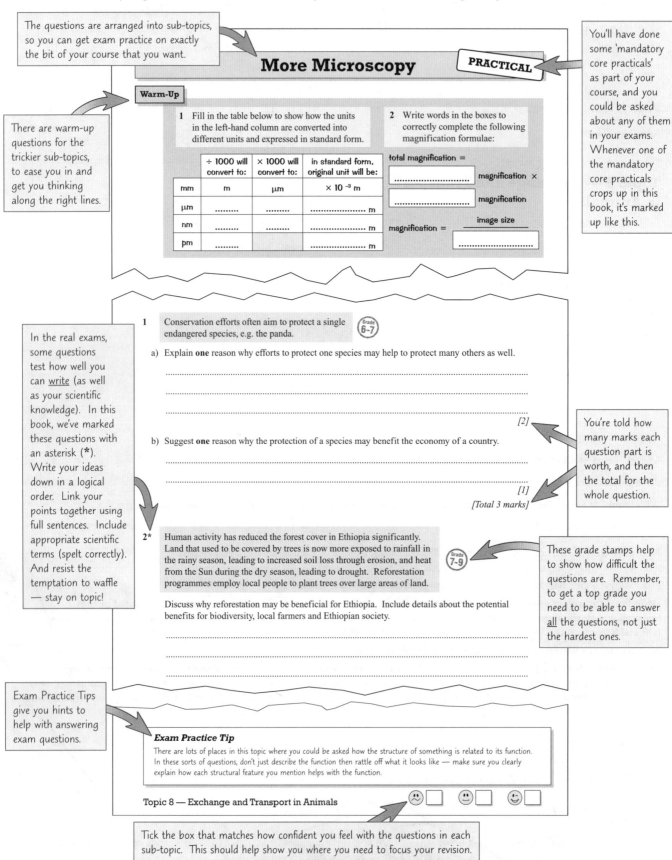

The questions are arranged into sub-topics, so you can get exam practice on exactly the bit of your course that you want.

There are warm-up questions for the trickier sub-topics, to ease you in and get you thinking along the right lines.

More Microscopy PRACTICAL

You'll have done some 'mandatory core practicals' as part of your course, and you could be asked about any of them in your exams. Whenever one of the mandatory core practicals crops up in this book, it's marked up like this.

Warm-Up

1 Fill in the table below to show how the units in the left-hand column are converted into different units and expressed in standard form.

	÷ 1000 will convert to:	× 1000 will convert to:	in standard form, original unit will be:
mm	m	μm	× 10⁻³ m
μm	....	....	.... m
nm	....	....	.... m
pm	....	....	.... m

2 Write words in the boxes to correctly complete the following magnification formulae:

total magnification =

.... magnification ×

.... magnification

magnification = image size / ....

In the real exams, some questions test how well you can <u>write</u> (as well as your scientific knowledge). In this book, we've marked these questions with an asterisk (*). Write your ideas down in a logical order. Link your points together using full sentences. Include appropriate scientific terms (spelt correctly). And resist the temptation to waffle — stay on topic!

1 Conservation efforts often aim to protect a single endangered species, e.g. the panda. [Grade 6-7]

a) Explain **one** reason why efforts to protect one species may help to protect many others as well.

....
....
....
[2]

b) Suggest **one** reason why the protection of a species may benefit the economy of a country.

....
....
[1]
[Total 3 marks]

You're told how many marks each question part is worth, and then the total for the whole question.

2* Human activity has reduced the forest cover in Ethiopia significantly. Land that used to be covered by trees is now more exposed to rainfall in the rainy season, leading to increased soil loss through erosion, and heat from the Sun during the dry season, leading to drought. Reforestation programmes employ local people to plant trees over large areas of land. [Grade 7-9]

Discuss why reforestation may be beneficial for Ethiopia. Include details about the potential benefits for biodiversity, local farmers and Ethiopian society.

....
....
....

These grade stamps help to show how difficult the questions are. Remember, to get a top grade you need to be able to answer <u>all</u> the questions, not just the hardest ones.

Exam Practice Tips give you hints to help with answering exam questions.

Exam Practice Tip
There are lots of places in this topic where you could be asked how the structure of something is related to its function. In these sorts of questions, don't just describe the function then rattle off what it looks like — make sure you clearly explain how each structural feature you mention helps with the function.

Topic 8 — Exchange and Transport in Animals ☹ ☐   ☺ ☐   ☺ ☐

Tick the box that matches how confident you feel with the questions in each sub-topic. This should help show you where you need to focus your revision.

Cells

Use the words on the right to correctly fill in the gaps in the passage.
You don't have to use every word, but each word can only be used once.

single
complex
multi
plant
animal
bacterial
simple

Eukaryotic cells include ...**animal**... and ...**plant**... cells.

Prokaryotic cells are smaller and more ...**simple**... than eukaryotic

cells. All prokaryotes are ...**single**...-celled organisms.

1 **Figure 1** shows a diagram of a plant cell.

Figure 1

a) Label the cell wall and the vacuole
on **Figure 1**.

[1]

b) Give the function of the following
subcellular structures:

Chloroplast **contains chlorophill that traps sunlight for photosynthesis**

Cell wall **keeps cell rigid, supports cell and strengthens it**

[2]

[Total 3 marks]

2 **Figure 2** shows a diagram of *Pseudomonas aeruginosa*, a type of bacterium.

Figure 2

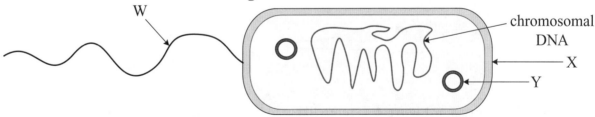

a) Name structures W, X, and Y on **Figure 2**.

W **Flagellum**

X **Cell wall**

Y **plasmid**

[3]

b) What is the function of the chromosomal DNA?

Contains most of the cells genetic information. Controls cells activities

[1]

[Total 4 marks]

3 Proteins are synthesised within cells. This is done when information from genes is used to join together a sequence of amino acids. The second half of the process is called translation.

Grade 4-6

a) Name **one** subcellular structure where genes are found within:

i) eukaryotic cells.

Nucleus

[1]

ii) prokaryotic cells.

Chromosomal DNA

[1]

b) Name the subcellular structure involved in the translation of genetic material in protein synthesis.

Ribosomes

[1]

c) Once proteins have been synthesised, they may need to leave the cell.
Name the subcellular structure that controls which substances leave the cell.

Cell membrane

[1]

[Total 4 marks]

4 **Figure 3** and **4** are diagrams of two different types of specialised cell.
One is a muscle cell and the other is a skin cell. They are not drawn to scale.

Grade 7-9

Figure 4

Figure 3

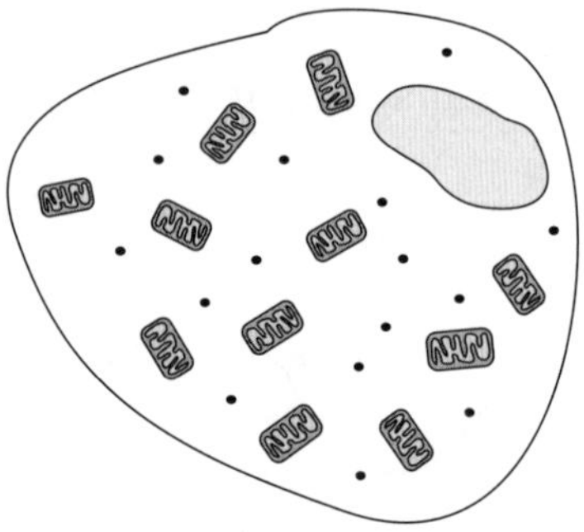

Which cell, **Figure 3** or **Figure 4**, is more likely to be a muscle cell? Explain your answer.

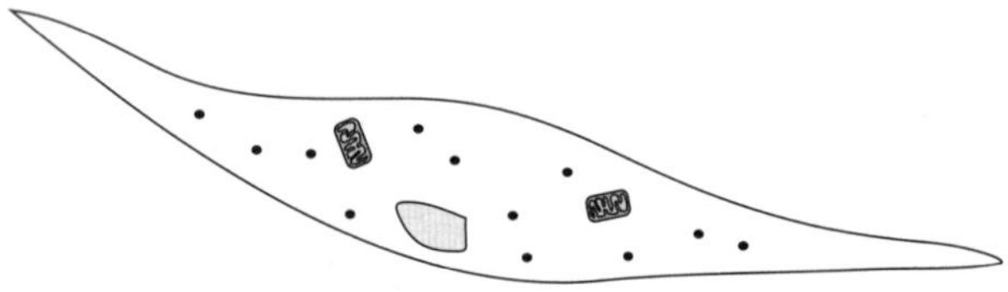

4 3 as 4 is quie big in comparison and contains lots of mitochondria to create energy for the muscles whereas 3 contains little mitochondria as a skin cell does not need much energy

[Total 4 marks]

Exam Practice Tip

Make sure you really know the difference between the structures of plant and animal cells (both eukaryotes) and bacterial cells (prokaryotes). Learn all the subcellular structures each one contains and the function of each of those parts — then you should be well-prepared for whatever cell-based questions the examiners throw at you.

Topic 1 — Key Concepts in Biology

Specialised Cells

1 An egg cell is fertilised when the nucleus of an egg cell and the nucleus of a sperm cell fuse together. Both egg cells and sperm cells are haploid. *(Grade 4-6)*

a) Elephant body cells contain 56 chromosomes.
How many chromosomes will an elephant egg cell contain?

28

[1]

b) Describe the role of a sperm's acrosome in fertilisation.

contains enzymes that digest the eggs membrane so it can fuse with it's nucleus

[2]

c) i) Explain why the membrane of an egg cell changes its structure immediately after fertilisation.

it becomes hard so only one sperm cell can enter it to fertilise it

[2]

ii) Explain how the cytoplasm of an egg cell is adapted to its function.

It has nutrients for the embryo

[1]

[Total 6 marks]

2 **Figure 1** shows a type of specialised cell which can be found in the lining of the fallopian tubes in the female reproductive system. *(Grade 6-7)*

Figure 1

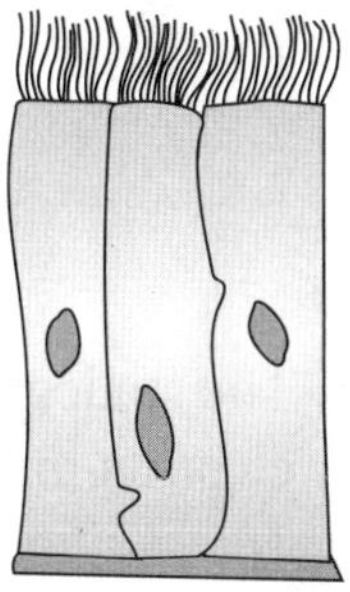

a) What is the name of this type of cell?

Epithilated

[1]

b) When an egg cell is ready to be fertilised, it moves through the fallopian tubes towards the uterus. Explain how the cells shown in **Figure 1** might be involved in this process.

The tiny membrane folds sweep the egg towards the uterus as it is contracted and so moves

[2]

[Total 3 marks]

Microscopy

1 A student wants to use a light microscope to view a sample of onion cells. **Figure 1** shows a diagram of the light microscope that she plans to use.

Grade 4-6

a) i) The three different objective lenses are labelled in **Figure 1** with their magnification. Which lens should the student select first when viewing her cells?

x4

....

[1]

Figure 1

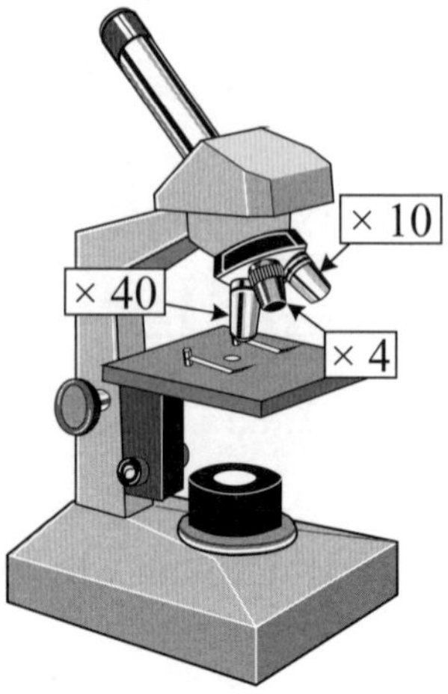

× 10

× 40

× 4

ii) After she has selected the objective lens, she looks down the eyepiece and uses the adjustment knobs. Describe the purpose of the adjustment knobs.

Fine focus

....

....

[1]

iii) The student wants to see the cells at a greater magnification. Describe the steps that she should take.

change the objective lens to a higher magnification
after starting on the smallest

....

[2]

b) After she has viewed the cells, she wants to produce a scientific drawing of them. Her teacher has advised her to use smooth lines to draw the structures she can see. Give **two** other ways in which she can ensure she produces an accurate and useful drawing.

1. *Do not shade*

2. *coth Do not overlap*

[2]

c) The student compares the image that she can see with an image of onion cells viewed with an electron microscope. Suggest how the two images would differ. Explain your answer.

Electron one will have more detail as the resolution
is higher. You will also see more structures
due to its greater magnification

....

[3]

[Total 9 marks]

Topic 1 — Key Concepts in Biology

More Microscopy

Warm-Up

1   Fill in the table below to show how the units in the left-hand column are converted into different units and expressed in standard form.

	÷ 1000 will convert to:	× 1000 will convert to:	in standard form, original unit will be:
mm	m	μm	$\times 10^{-3}$ m
μm	*mm*	*nm*	......$\times 10^{-6}$...... m
nm	*μm*	*pm*	......$\times 10^{-9}$...... m
pm	*nm*		......$\times 10^{-12}$...... m

2   Write words in the boxes to correctly complete the following magnification formulae:

total magnification =

......*eyepiece*...... magnification ×

......*objective*...... magnification

$$\text{magnification} = \frac{\text{image size}}{......actual......}$$

1   **Figure 1** shows an image of a sample of epithelial cells viewed using a light microscope. An eyepiece lens with a magnification of × 10 and an objective lens with a magnification of × 100 were used to view the cells.

Grade 6-7

Figure 1

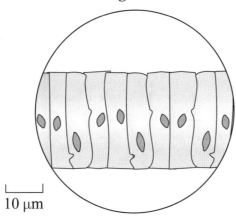

10 μm

a) i) Calculate the total magnification used to view the cells.

1000

total magnification = ...1000......
[1]

ii) Estimate the average height of the cells.

3

average height of the cells = ...3...... μm
[1]

b) A student examines another cell type at the same magnification and finds its average height to be 8 μm. This can be expressed in standard form as

☑ **A** 8×10^{-6} m ☐ **B** 0.8×10^{-6} m ☐ **C** 8×10^{-12} m ☐ **D** 0.8×10^{-12} m
[1]

[Total 3 marks]

Topic 1 — Key Concepts in Biology

2   A student observed blood cells under a microscope.
A scale drawing of one of the cells is shown in **Figure 2**.

Figure 2

A

a) **A** is the cell width. The real width of **A** is 0.012 mm.
Calculate the magnification of the image.

$\frac{A}{0.012}$

magnification = ...
[2]

b) The cell is then viewed with a magnification of × **400**.
Calculate the new width of the image in mm.

400 × 0.012

width of image = ...4.8................ mm
[2]

[Total 4 marks]

3   A plant cell is magnified 1000 times under a light microscope.
The length of the image of the plant cell is 10 mm.

a) Calculate the actual length of the plant cell in μm.

10 000

actual length of plant cell = ... μm
[3]

b) An electron microscope is used to look inside the cell in more detail.
A virus particle is noticed that measures 4 × 10⁻⁵ mm in width.
Calculate the width of the virus in nm.

40

.... nm
[3]

[Total 6 marks]

Exam Practice Tip

Microscopy questions can include some pretty tricky maths. Make sure you learn the magnification formulae and know
how to convert from one unit of length to another. Then there's standard form to master — make sure you understand
the value of a number written in standard form and can use numbers written in standard form in calculations. Phew.

7

Enzymes

1 Enzymes are biological catalysts. (Grade 4-6)

a) State how a catalyst affects the rate of a reaction.

Speeds it up without beg being used up

[1]

b) Name the part of an enzyme where substrate molecules bind.

Active Site

[1]

c) Enzymes have a 'high specificity' for their substrate. Describe what this means.

They will only bind to a specific substrate due to their shape

[1]

[Total 3 marks]

2 The concentration of substrate molecules affects the rate of an enzyme-controlled reaction. (Grade 6-7)

a) Which of the graphs below (**A**, **B**, **C** or **D**) correctly shows how the rate of an enzyme-controlled reaction is affected by substrate concentration?

☑ **A**

C ☐

B ☐

D ☐

[1]

b) Explain why increasing the substrate concentration fails to affect the rate of an enzyme-controlled reaction after a certain point.

All the active sites are full so the rate of reaction is constant

[2]

[Total 3 marks]

Topic 1 — Key Concepts in Biology

3 Temperature affects the rate of enzyme activity. Enzyme A has an optimum temperature of 38 °C. **Figure 1** shows enzyme A before and after being exposed to a temperature of 60 °C.

Figure 1

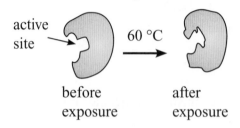

active
site

60 °C

before
exposure

after
exposure

Enzyme A's activity will be different at 38 °C and 60 °C. Explain why.

....

....

....

....

[Total 3 marks]

4 A scientist investigated the effect of pH on the activity of an enzyme by calculating the rate of reaction for several pH values. His results are shown in **Figure 2**.

Figure 2

pH	3.6	3.8	4.0	4.4	4.8	5.0	5.2
Rate (cm³ s⁻¹)	2.0	5.0	8.0	11.0	8.0	4.0	1.0

a) i) Use the grid in **Figure 3** to draw a graph using the values in **Figure 2**. Include a curve of best fit.

[2]

ii) Determine the optimum pH for this enzyme.

....

[1]

b) Describe and explain the effect on enzyme activity of increasing the pH above the optimum level.

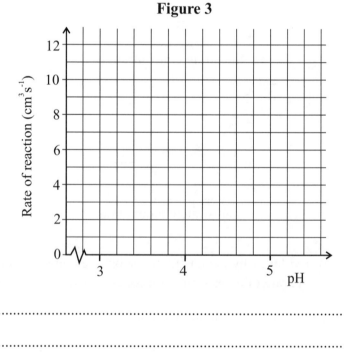

Figure 3

Rate of reaction (cm³ s⁻¹)

12

10

8

6

4

2

0

3   4   5
                          pH

....

....

....

....

[3]

[Total 6 marks]

Topic 1 — Key Concepts in Biology

More on Enzymes

1 The enzyme amylase is involved in the breakdown of starch into simple sugars.

A student investigated the effect of pH on the activity of amylase in starch solution. Amylase and starch solution were added to test tubes X, Y and Z. A different buffer solution was added to each test tube. Each buffer solution had a different pH value, as shown in **Figure 1**. Spotting tiles were prepared with a drop of iodine solution in each well. Iodine solution is a browny-orange colour but it turns blue-black in the presence of starch.

Figure 1

Test tube	pH
X	4
Y	6
Z	11

Every 30 seconds a drop of the solution from each of the test tubes was added to a separate well on a spotting tile. The resulting colour of the solution in the well was recorded as shown in **Figure 2**.

Figure 2

Time (s)	30	60	90	120	150
Tube X	Blue-black	Blue-black	Blue-black	Browny-orange	Browny-orange
Tube Y	Blue-black	Browny-orange	Browny-orange	Browny-orange	Browny-orange
Tube Z	Blue-black	Blue-black	Blue-black	Blue-black	Blue-black

a) State the pH at which the rate of reaction was greatest. Explain your answer.

....

....

....

[2]

b) Suggest an explanation for the results in tube **Z**.

....

....

[1]

c) i) In any experiment, it is important to control the variables that are not being tested. State how the student could control the temperature in the test tubes.

....

[1]

ii) Give **two** other variables that should be controlled in this experiment.

1. ....

2. ....

[2]

d) The student repeated her experiment at pH 7 and got the same results as she got for her experiment at pH 6. Describe how she could improve her experiment to find whether the reaction is greatest at pH 6 or 7.

....

....

[1]

[Total 7 marks]

Topic 1 — Key Concepts in Biology

Enzymes in Breakdown and Synthesis

1   **Figure 1** shows how different molecules are broken down by enzymes.

Figure 1

carbohydrate → A → simple sugars   B → protease → C

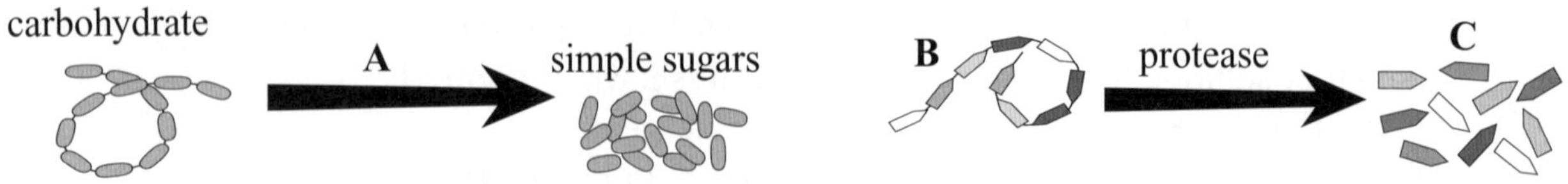

a) Name the molecules labelled A-C in **Figure 1**.

A ....

B ....

C ....

[3]

b) Explain why the breakdown of large molecules into smaller components is necessary
   for organisms.

....

....

....

[2]

[Total 5 marks]

2   Orlistat is a drug that is used to help lower obesity rates.
     It works by preventing lipase from working in the digestive system.

Explain why patients taking Orlistat may have oily faeces.

....

....

....

....

....

[Total 3 marks]

Exam Practice Tip

Examiners tend to like asking questions about enzymes — that's because they can make you draw together lots of your
knowledge in a single question. For example, you might get asked how temperature affects the breakdown of lipids —
you'd need to know that lipases are enzymes which breakdown lipids <u>and</u> how temperature affects enzyme activity.

Testing for Biological Molecules [PRACTICAL]

Warm-Up

Draw lines to connect the tests on the left with the biological molecules that they identify.

| Biuret test | | Lipids | | Proteins |

Benedict's test

Emulsion test   Iodine test

Starch   Reducing sugars

1   A student is analysing the nutrient content of egg whites.   (Grade 4-6)

a) Describe a test the student could do to find out if fat is present in a sample of the egg whites.

....

....

....

[4]

b) Describe how the student could test for protein in a sample of the egg whites.

....

....

....

[3]

[Total 7 marks]

2   A student was given test tubes containing the following glucose concentrations: (Grade 6-7)
0 M, 0.02 M, 0.1 M, 1 M. The test tubes were not labelled and he was asked to
perform tests to determine which test tube contained which glucose solution.

a) Describe the test he could carry out to try to distinguish between the glucose solutions.

....

....

....

[3]

b) **Figure 1** shows the substance observed in the test tubes following his tests. Complete **Figure 1** to
show which glucose solution (0 M, 0.02 M, 0.1 M, 1 M) each test tube contained.

Figure 1

	Tube 1	Tube 2	Tube 3	Tube 4
substance observed	yellow precipitate	blue solution	red precipitate	green precipitate
glucose concentration (M)	....	....	....	....

[1]

[Total 4 marks]

Topic 1 — Key Concepts in Biology

Energy in Food

1 A student wanted to measure the amount of energy in a number of different foods. They burned a sample of each food under a boiling tube containing 20 cm³ of water and measured the temperature of the water before and after the food was burned.

Grade 7-9

a) State the name given to this method for finding the energy content of food.

....

[1]

b) The results of the student's experiment are shown in **Figure 1**.
Calculate the energy content in joules of the crisp.
Use the equation: energy (J) = mass of water (g) × temperature change of water (°C) × 4.2

Figure 1

energy content of crisp = ... J

[2]

c) Calculate the energy content of the rice in J per gram.

Food	Crisp	Rice	Marsh-mallow
Mass of food (g)	0.20	0.56	0.24
Temperature of water before burning (°C)	20.0	19.8	19.9
Temperature of water after burning (°C)	49.0	42.3	48.5
Energy in food (J)	....	1890	2402

energy content of rice = ... J/g

[1]

d) Give **one** variable that the student should control in the experiment.

....

[1]

e) The nutritional information on the packet of marshmallows states that there are 1300 kJ per 100 g.

i) Calculate the kJ per 100 g in the marshmallows based on the student's experiment.
Give your answer to 2 decimal places.

energy content of marshmallows .... kJ/100 g

[3]

ii) Explain why the student's result is different from the true energy content of the marshmallows stated on the packet.

....

....

....

[1]

[Total 9 marks]

Diffusion, Osmosis and Active Transport

Warm-Up

The diagram on the right shows three cells. The carbon dioxide concentration inside each cell is shown. Draw arrows between the cells to show in which directions the carbon dioxide will diffuse.

> carbon dioxide concentration = 0.2%
>
> carbon dioxide concentration = 1.5%
>
> carbon dioxide concentration = 3.0% ← cell

---

1 The cell membrane is important in controlling what substances can enter or leave a cell. **Grade 4-6**

a) Describe the process of diffusion.

....

....

[2]

b) Which of these molecules is too large to diffuse through a cell membrane?

☐ **A** protein

☐ **B** oxygen

☐ **C** glucose

☐ **D** water

[1]

[Total 3 marks]

2 Osmosis is a form of diffusion. **Grade 4-6**

a) In which **one** of these scenarios is osmosis occurring?

☐ **A** Water is moving from the mouth down into the stomach.

☐ **B** Sugar is being taken up into the blood from the gut.

☐ **C** A plant is absorbing water from the soil.

☐ **D** Oxygen is entering the blood from the lungs.

[1]

b) Give the definition of osmosis.

....

....

....

[2]

[Total 3 marks]

Topic 1 — Key Concepts in Biology

14

3 Diffusion, osmosis and active transport all involve the movement of molecules.

(Grade 6-7)

Draw arrows in the boxes underneath **Figure 1** to illustrate the direction of the net movement of the following:

Figure 1

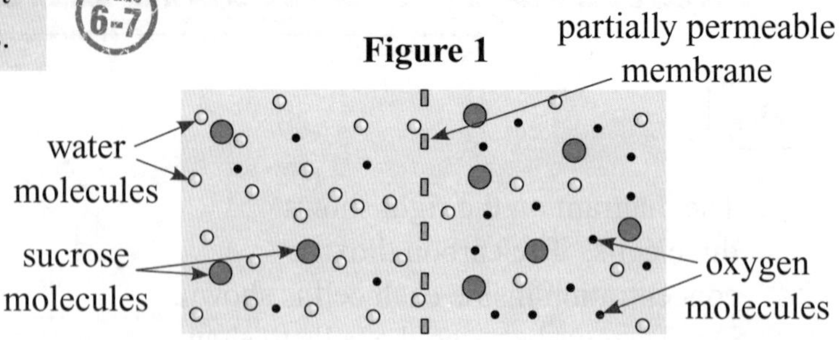

partially permeable membrane

water molecules

sucrose molecules

oxygen molecules

a) sucrose molecules moving by active transport:

[1]

b) water molecules moving by osmosis:

[1]

c) oxygen molecules moving by diffusion:

[1]

[Total 3 marks]

4 Amino acids are absorbed in the gut by active transport. **Figure 2** shows a diagram of amino acids being absorbed into the bloodstream across the epithelial cells of the gut.

(Grade 6-7)

Figure 2

A

epithelial cell

BLOODSTREAM

GUT

amino acids

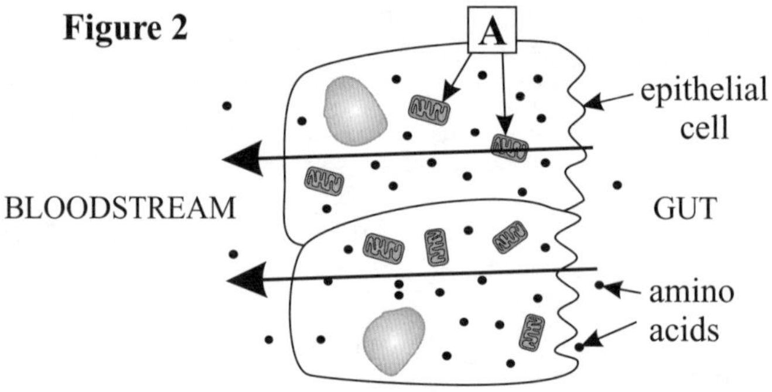

a) Using **Figure 2**, explain why active transport is necessary for the absorption of amino acids into the bloodstream.

....

....

....

....

[3]

b) Explain why the subcellular structures labelled **A** on **Figure 2** are needed in this process.

....

....

....

[2]

[Total 5 marks]

Investigating Osmosis

1   A student investigated the effect of different sucrose solutions on pieces of potato. He cut five equal-sized chips from a potato, and measured and recorded the mass of each. Each potato chip was placed in a beaker containing a different concentration of sucrose solution. The mass of the chips was measured after one hour, and the percentage change in mass of each chip was then calculated. The results are shown in **Figure 1**.

a) The mass of the potato chip in Beaker 5 was 10.0 g before the experiment and 9.3 g afterwards. Calculate the percentage change in mass of the potato chip in Beaker 5.

Figure 1

	Beaker				
	1	2	3	4	5
Concentration of sucrose solution (M)	0.1	0.3	0.5	0.7	0.9
% change in mass of potato chip	9	2	–3	–6	....

Change in mass = ... %

[1]

b) Explain what caused the increase in mass of the potato chips in Beakers 1 and 2.

....

....

[2]

c) Draw a graph of concentration of sucrose solution against percentage change in mass on the grid in **Figure 2**. Include a curve of best fit.

Figure 2

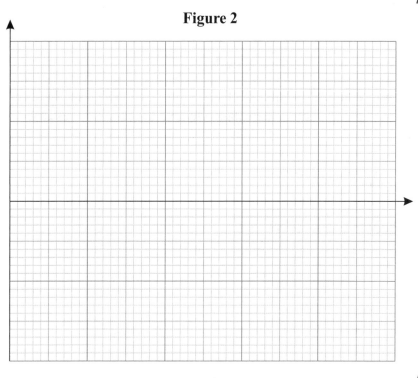

[4]

d) The student wanted to find a concentration of sucrose that would not cause the mass of the potato chip to change. Describe how the student could do this using the graph of the results.

....

....

[1]

[Total 8 marks]

Topic 1 — Key Concepts in Biology

Topic 2 — Cells and Control

Mitosis

1 Damaged skin tissue can be repaired by mitosis. *(Grade 6-7)*

a) Describe what happens in each of these stages of mitosis:

Prophase ....

....

Telophase ....

....

[4]

b) The new skin cells produced by mitosis will be:

☐ **A** Diploid and genetically identical to each other.

☐ **C** Diploid and genetically different to each other.

☐ **B** Haploid and genetically identical to each other.

☐ **D** Haploid and genetically different to each other.

[1]

c) Other than tissue repair, give **one** reason why an organism's cells divide by mitosis.

....

[1]

[Total 6 marks]

2 Mitosis is part of the cell cycle. *(Grade 6-7)*

a) Before mitosis occurs, a cell goes through interphase. Describe what happens to the cell's DNA during interphase and explain why this process is necessary.

....

....

[2]

b) **Figure 1** shows a cell undergoing mitosis.

Figure 1

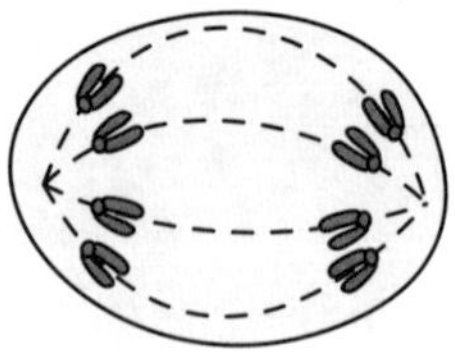

i) Name the stage of mitosis that the cell is going through.

....

[1]

ii) Describe what is happening during this stage.

....

....

[2]

c) The cell cycle is not complete until cytokinesis has occurred.
Describe what happens during cytokinesis.

....

[1]

[Total 6 marks]

Cell Division and Growth

1   **Figure 1** shows a flowering plant.   (Grade 4-6)

Figure 1

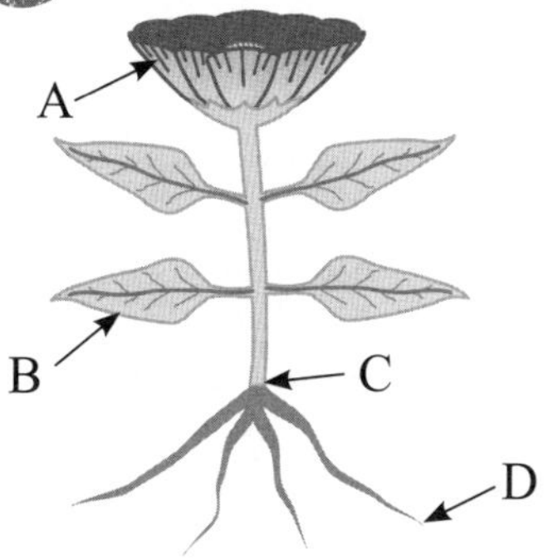

a)   Which label (**A-D**) shows a site where growth usually occurs by cell division?

☐   **A**   ☐   **B**   ☐   **C**   ☐   **D**

[1]

b)   Name the main process by which plants grow in height.

....

[1]

[Total 2 marks]

2   Animals start life as embryos, which grow and develop.   (Grade 6-7)

a)   State the purpose of cell differentiation in an animal embryo.

....

[1]

b)   Describe **two** differences between the growth of animals and the growth of plants.

1. ....

....

2. ....

....

[2]

[Total 3 marks]

3   A tumour can occur in any organ in the body. Not all tumours are cancerous.   (Grade 6-7)

a)   Explain how a tumour forms.

....

....

....

[3]

b)   Describe the point at which a tumour is classed as a cancer.

....

[1]

[Total 4 marks]

4 Percentile charts are used to record and monitor a child's growth.

a) A child's mass was recorded regularly and plotted on the percentile chart shown in **Figure 2**. The crosses represent the child's mass.

i) Explain what the line labelled '25th' on the chart represents.

....

....

....

....
[2]

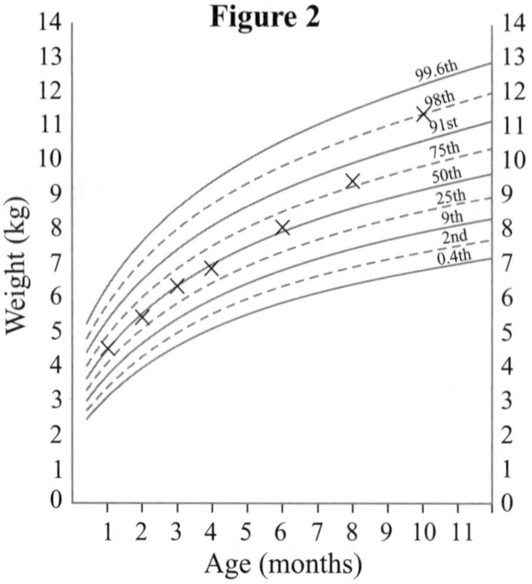

ii) Describe the growth trend shown on the chart and suggest why a doctor might be concerned about the child's growth.

....

....

....

....

....
[3]

Figure 2

Weight (kg) vs Age (months). Percentile lines labelled 99.6th, 98th, 91st, 75th, 50th, 25th, 9th, 2nd, 0.4th.

b) Give **two** other measurements that could be plotted on a percentile chart to monitor growth.

1. ....   2. ....
[2]

[Total 7 marks]

5 **Figure 3** shows the mass of an animal plotted against its age in weeks.

a) Calculate the rate of growth between 0 and 60 weeks. Give your answer to 2 significant figures.

rate of growth = ... kg week^{-1}
[2]

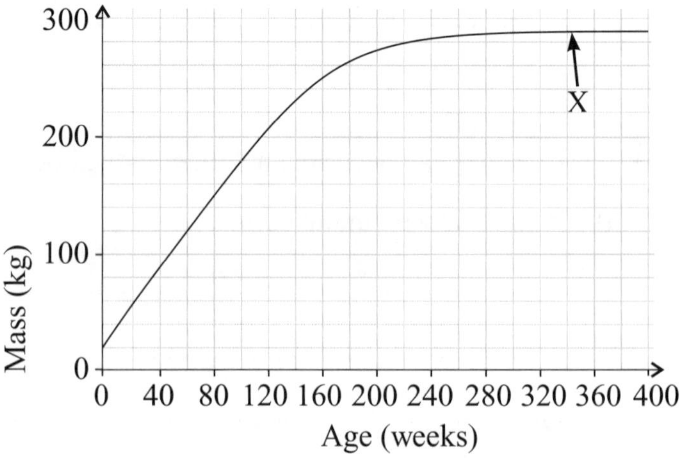

b) The animal reaches full growth at 300 weeks. Comment on the amount of cell differentiation you'd expect to be occurring at the point marked **X** on the graph. Explain your answer.

Figure 3

Mass (kg) vs Age (weeks), with point X marked near 360 weeks.

....

....

....
[2]

[Total 4 marks]

Topic 2 — Cells and Control

Stem Cells

Warm-Up

Circle the correct words shown in bold to complete the passage below.

Stem cells are able to **differentiate** / **mutate** to become **specialised** / **unspecialised** cells.

Stem cells found in **adults** / **early human embryos** can produce any type of cell at all.

In plants, stem cells are found in areas of the plant that are **growing** / **photosynthesising**.

Plant stem cells can produce **only a small number of cell types** / **any cell type**.

1   Scientists can use stem cells to grow new cells, which they can then use to test new drugs on.   **Grade 4-6**

a) Stem cells are

☐ **A** gametes   ☐ **B** specialised   ☐ **C** undifferentiated   ☐ **D** differentiated

[1]

b) i) Explain **one** reason why scientists may prefer to use embryonic stem cells for research rather than adult stem cells.

....

....

[2]

ii) Suggest **one** reason why people are against research involving embryonic stem cells.

....

[1]

c) Scientists can also use plant stem cells in drug research.
Name the plant tissue that produces stem cells.

....

[1]

[Total 5 marks]

2   Scientists are researching whether it's possible to use embryonic stem cells to produce insulin-secreting cells, which could potentially be implanted in a patient in order to cure them of type 1 diabetes.   **Grade 7-9**

Explain **two** potential risks of using stem cells to cure type 1 diabetes.

....

....

....

....

....

[Total 4 marks]

Topic 2 — Cells and Control

The Brain and Spinal Cord

1 **Figure 1** shows the human brain. *(Grade 6-7)*

Figure 1

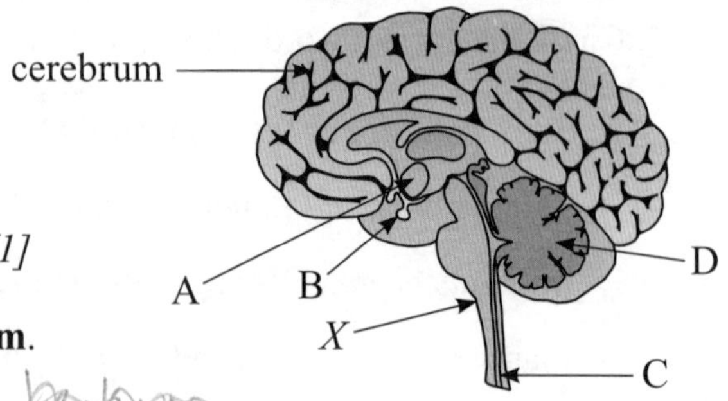

a) Which letter on **Figure 1** (**A**, **B**, **C** or **D**) shows the **cerebellum**?

☐ **A**   ☐ **B**   ☐ **C**   ☑ **D**

[1]

b) Describe the structure and function of the **cerebrum**.

2 hemispheres that contol balance
and precise movement voluntary Movement, senses,
memory

[2]

c) Some drugs affect the function of the structure labelled **X** on **Figure 1**. Explain why these drugs could be fatal if taken in excess.

X is the medulla oblongata which contols
unconcious reactions like heart rate so if it is
affected, heart rate can be affected - which could
be fatal

[2]

[Total 5 marks]

2 Medical scanners can be used to investigate brain function. *(Grade 6-7)*

A doctor arranged for her patient to have a CT scan.
The patient had been experiencing episodes of clumsiness and difficulty walking.

a) i) The patient was found to have a tumour in her brain. Suggest the area of the brain in which the tumour was found. Give a reason for your answer.

Cerebellum as it contols balance

[2]

ii) Give **one** reason why brain tumours can be difficult to treat.

It is hard to surgically remove tumours in certain
parts of the brain

[1]

b) PET scans can also be used to investigate brain function. Give **two** differences between CT scans and PET scans.

1. PET shows structure and function
2. PET uses radioactive chemicals

[2]

[Total 5 marks]

Topic 2 — Cells and Control

The Nervous System

Use the words below to complete the following sentences about the nervous system. Each word can only be used once.

motor	sensory	receptors	effectors

The body has lots of sensory ....*receptors*........ , which detect environmental stimuli.

When this happens, nervous impulses are sent along .....*sensory*.............. neurones to

the central nervous system. From the central nervous system, impulses are sent along

..........*motor*.............. neurones to .....*effectors*............ , which produce a response.

---

1 Motor neurone disease occurs when motor neurones stop working as they should. **Grade 7-9**

a) **Figure 1** shows a motor neurone.

Figure 1

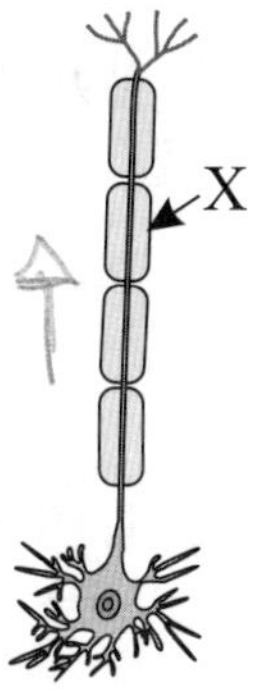

i) Add an arrow to **Figure 1** to show the direction a nervous impulse would travel along the neurone.

[1]

ii) Name the part labelled **X** and describe its function.

......*Myelin sheath - insulates the neurone so electrical*
impulse is not lost electrical insulator and
speeds up impulse
[2]

iii) Describe **two** structural differences between a motor neurone and a sensory neurone.

1. ......*Sensory has cell body in the middle*..............

....

2. ......*Sensory has long dendron*.............................

....
[2]

b) Explain why a person with motor neurone disease may have difficulty swallowing.

......*Motor neurone sends impulses to the effector to produce a*
response so if they have a problem with motor neurones
the impulses may not be sent to effector controlling [2]
swallowing

c) A motor neurone is 58 cm long. An impulse travels along it at 110 m s^{-1}.
Calculate how long it would take the impulse to travel the length of the neurone in milliseconds. Give your answer to 3 significant figures.

d

s   t

.... ms
[3]
[Total 10 marks]

Synapses and Reflexes

1 Humans have many different reflexes. (Grade 4-6)

a) Reflexes are

☐ **A** slow and under conscious control   ☑ **C** rapid and automatic

☐ **B** rapid and under conscious control   ☐ **D** slow and automatic

[1]

b) **Figure 1** shows a diagram of a reflex arc.

Figure 1

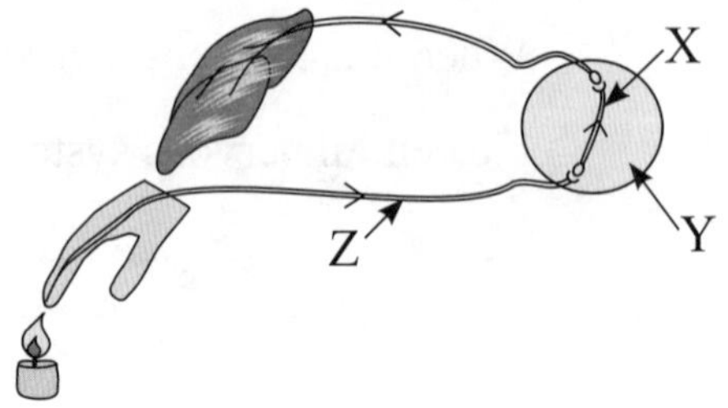

i) Name the structure labelled **X**.

Relay neurone

[1]

ii) Name **two** parts of the body that the part of the diagram labelled **Y** could represent.

1. Spinal cord

2. Unconscious part of brain

[2]

iii) Name the structure labelled **Z** and describe its function.

Sensory neurone - sends impulses to effector to cross synapse relay neurone from receptor

[2]

iv) State the purpose of the reflex arc shown in **Figure 1**.

To move hand from fire

[1]

[Total 7 marks]

2 Some stimuli are interpreted by the brain as being painful. When receptors detect these stimuli, impulses are passed to the spinal cord and then to the brain. Opioid drugs can relieve pain, partly because they prevent the release of neurotransmitters from certain sensory neurones.

With reference to synapses, explain how opioids can relieve pain. (Grade 7-9)

....

....

....

....

[Total 3 marks]

Exam Practice Tip

The pathway that nervous impulses take in a reflex arc is always the same — receptor, sensory neurone, relay neurone (in the spinal cord or an unconscious part of the brain), motor neurone, effector. Learn this pathway (and understand that synapses connect neurones) then you'll be able to tackle any exam question on reflexes, even if it's a reflex you've not learnt.

Topic 2 — Cells and Control

The Eye

Use the words below to correctly label the diagram of the eye.
You don't have to use every word, but each word can only be used once.

| iris | pupil | cornea | lens | optic nerve | retina |

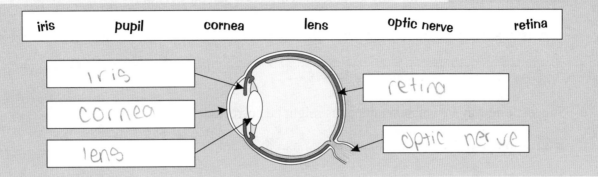

iris

cornea

lens

retina

optic nerve

1   The eye is an organ containing receptors. Grade 4-6

a) i) Which part of the eye contains receptor cells that are sensitive to light?

rods in the retina

[1]

ii) Name the **two** types of receptor cell in the eye and briefly describe the role of each type.

1. rods ~ sensitive to light

2. cones ~ sensitive to colour

[2]

iii) Describe how red-green colour-blindness is caused.

Problem with cones (red or green)

[1]

b) Describe the function of the iris.

Controls size of pupil to let in more or less light   how much light is let into pupil

[1]

[Total 5 marks]

2   Cataracts are a very common cause of blurred vision. Grade 4-6

a) Explain why cataracts prevent a person from seeing clearly.

Clouds the lens

[2]

b) Describe how cataracts can be treated.   Artificial

Replacing lens with a prostic one

[1]

[Total 3 marks]

3 Keratoconus is a condition where the cornea gets thinner and changes shape. **(Grade 6-7)**

a) Describe the function of the cornea.

Bends light into the eye

[1]

b) Suggest an explanation for why keratoconus affects a person's vision.

Light is not bent to the retina to detect the
light and colour to create an image

[2]

c) Suggest **one** way in which keratoconus might be corrected.

Laser eye surgery

[1]

[Total 4 marks]

4 **Figure 1** shows a man using glasses to correct his long-sightedness. **(Grade 6-7)**

Figure 1

a) i) Describe where light is brought into focus in the eye of a person who is long-sighted.

Behind the retina

[1]

ii) Explain how long-sightedness can be treated with glasses.

Diverging lens

[2]

b) In people with normal vision, explain how the shape of the lens changes to allow
a person to see nearby objects clearly.

Ciliary muscles contracts , suspensory ligaments
slack, lens becomes more round ;light is
refracted more

[4]

[Total 7 marks]

Topic 2 — Cells and Control

Sexual Reproduction and Meiosis

1 Gametes are produced by meiosis. Human gametes are egg and sperm cells. (Grade 4-6)

a) Gametes contain...

☐ **A** ...twice as many chromosomes as other body cells.

☐ **B** ...a quarter of the number of chromosomes in other body cells.

☐ **C** ...three times as many chromosomes as other body cells.

☐ **D** ...half the number of chromosomes in other body cells.

[1]

b) Meiosis results in the production of...

☐ **A** ...two genetically identical daughter cells.

☐ **B** ...four genetically identical daughter cells.

☐ **C** ...two genetically different daughter cells.

☐ **D** ...four genetically different daughter cells.

[1]

c) State the name given to the cell formed from two gametes at fertilisation.

....

[1]

[Total 3 marks]

2 **Figure 1** shows a diploid cell about to undergo meiosis. (Grade 6-7)

Figure 1   **Figure 2**

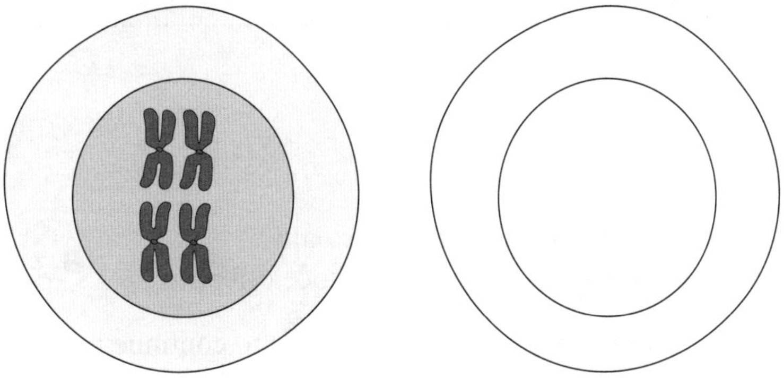

a) Complete **Figure 2** to show the number of chromosomes in a haploid gamete of this organism.

[2]

b) Explain why haploid gametes are necessary for sexual reproduction.

....

....

....

[2]

[Total 4 marks]

☹ ☐   ☺ ☐   ☺ ☐

Asexual and Sexual Reproduction

Warm-Up

Circle the correct underlined word to complete the following sentences.

Organisms reproduce in order to pass on their genes/cells.

Asexual reproduction usually involves cell division by meiosis/mitosis.
It results in genetically different/identical offspring.

Sexual reproduction involves cell division by meiosis/mitosis.
It results in genetically different/identical offspring.

1   In some species of stick insect, the female is able to lay eggs that
    hatch to produce offspring without the eggs being fertilised by a male.   Grade 4-6

a) Is this an example of sexual or asexual reproduction? Explain your answer.

....

....

[1]

b) Explain **one** advantage and **one** disadvantage of the female stick insect reproducing in this way.

Advantage: ....

....

Disadvantage: ....

....

[2]

[Total 3 marks]

2   Mint plants can reproduce both sexually and asexually,
    although sexual reproduction takes longer to produce offspring.   Grade 6-7

Explain why it may be more beneficial for mint plants to continue to
reproduce sexually, despite it taking longer to produce offspring.

....

....

....

....

....

[Total 3 marks]

DNA

1 Scientists have studied the human genome. (Grade 4-6)

a) What is a genome?

[✓] **A** All of an organism's DNA.   [ ] **C** All of an organism's genes.

[ ] **B** All of an organism's proteins.   [ ] **D** All of an organism's DNA and proteins.

[1]

b) The human genome contains over 20 000 genes.
Explain what is meant by the term 'gene'.

....

....

[1]

c) Describe how DNA is stored in the nucleus of eukaryotic cells.

....

....

[2]

[Total 4 marks]

2 **Figure 1** shows a section of a DNA double helix. (Grade 4-6)

Figure 1

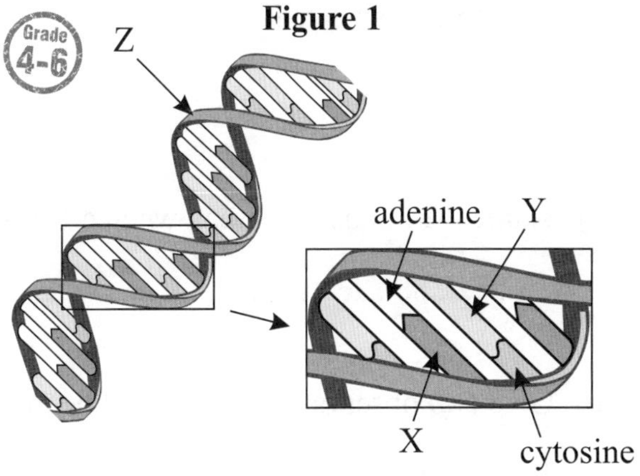

a) Name the bases labelled **X** and **Y** on **Figure 1**.

X: thymine

Y: Guanine

[2]

b) i) State the **two** components of the part of the
molecule labelled **Z** on **Figure 1**.

1. Phosphate group

2. sugar

[2]

ii) State which of these components has a base attached.

Sugar

[1]

c) DNA is a polymer. Explain what this means.

....

....

[1]

[Total 6 marks]

Topic 3 — Genetics

3 A student is extracting DNA from an apple. He begins by breaking up the apple using a food blender. He then adds an 'extraction solution' to the fruit pulp.

Grade
6-7

a) Apart from water, state **two** components of the 'extraction solution'.

1. .... 2. ....

[2]

b) The student filters the mixture into a boiling tube.
Explain what the student needs to do next to obtain a DNA precipitate.

....

....

....

[2]

[Total 4 marks]

4 When a DNA molecule denatures, the bonds between bases on opposite DNA strands break and the two strands separate. **Figure 2** shows how the percentage of denatured DNA in a sample changes as the sample is heated.

Grade
7-9

Figure 2

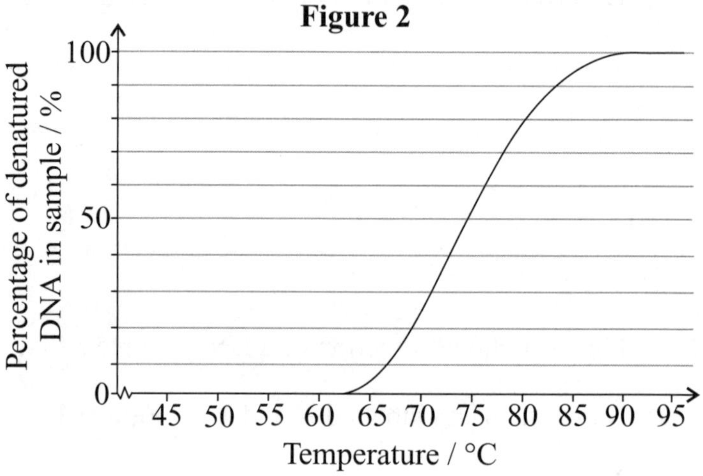

a) Name the bonds that break when a DNA molecule denatures.

....

[1]

b) Give **two** observations that could be made from the data in **Figure 2**.

1. ....

....

2. ....

....

[2]

c) The DNA sample above contains 8.14×10^4 base pairs.
Calculate how many base pairs have separated at 70 °C.
Give your answer in standard form to 3 significant figures.

.... base pairs

[2]

[Total 5 marks]

Protein Synthesis

1 A gene in a species of flowering plant codes for a protein that determines flower colour. **Figure 1** shows a sequence of bases in a section of this gene.

Grade 6-7

Figure 1

A	T	C	C	C	G	A	A	C	T	C	G	G	C

a) What is the maximum number of amino acids that can be coded for by this gene?

☐ **A** 6 ☐ **B** 5 ☐ **C** 4 ☑ **D** 3

[1]

b) A genetic variant of this gene is discovered.

i) Explain how the genetic variant will be different to the normal version of the gene.

....

....

[2]

ii) Explain how this genetic variant could change the phenotype of the plant.

....

....

....

....

....

[4]

[Total 7 marks]

2 **Figure 2** shows two different proteins in the human body. Collagen is a structural protein. It supports structures such as muscle tendons. Haemoglobin is a transport protein. It transports oxygen around the body.

Grade 7-9

Figure 2

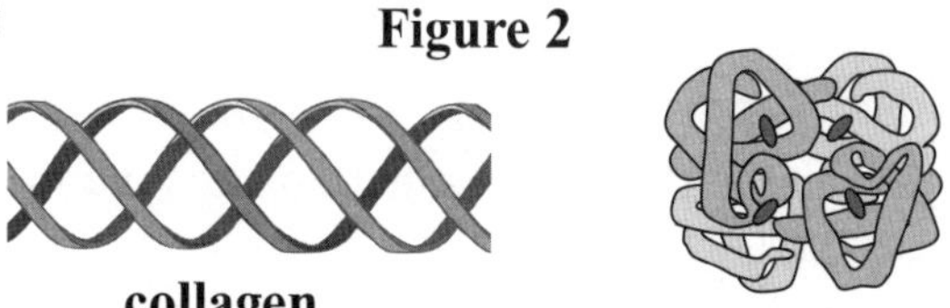

collagen

haemoglobin

With reference to genes, explain how it is possible for these two proteins to have such different functions.

....

....

....

....

....

[Total 4 marks]

More on Protein Synthesis

Use the words below to fill in the gaps in the passage about protein synthesis.
Not all of the words will be used.

ribosomes   translation   mitochondria   transcription   cytoplasm   translocation

In the first stage of protein synthesis, DNA is copied into mRNA.

This is called .... In the second stage of protein synthesis,

a protein is assembled according to the instructions in mRNA. This is called

.... It takes place in the ....

and is carried out by ....

1   To make a protein, the base sequence in the coding DNA of a gene is copied into mRNA.   **Grade 4-6**

a)   Which of the following sets of bases are found in mRNA?

☐ **A** A, T, C, G   ☐ **C** A, U, C, G

☐ **B** A, T, C, U   ☐ **D** A, E, C, G

[1]

b)   A set of three bases in mRNA is called:

☐ **A** an amino acid   ☐ **C** a gene

☐ **B** a codon   ☐ **D** a variant

[1]

c)   Name the part of the cell in which mRNA is made.

....

[1]

d)   Name the process that ensures the mRNA produced is a complementary copy of the gene.

....

[1]

e)   Describe the role of RNA polymerase in the production of mRNA.

....

[1]

f)   Explain the purpose of mRNA.

....

....

[2]

[Total 7 marks]

2   **Figure 2** shows a section of DNA containing coding and non-coding regions.

Figure 2

Non-coding   Gene (coding DNA)   Non-coding
DNA   DNA

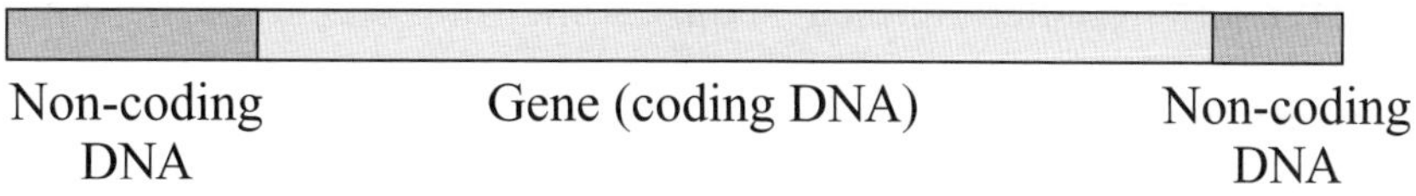

a)* Explain how a polypeptide (protein) would be produced from this section of DNA in a cell.

....

....

....

....

....

....

....

....

....

....

....

....

....

[6]

b) A mutation occurs in the non-coding region of DNA at the start of the gene.
Explain how this could result in fewer polypeptides being produced.

....

....

....

....

....

[3]

[Total 9 marks]

Exam Practice Tip

There's no doubt about it — protein synthesis is a tricky topic and there's an awful lot to remember here. The best way to learn it is to break it down into stages (transcription and translation) and then go over the steps involved in each stage in order, until you've grasped them. And remember, <u>m</u>RNA is the <u>m</u>essenger and <u>t</u>RNA <u>t</u>ransfers amino acids.

Topic 3 — Genetics

The Work of Mendel

1 Mendel was a 19th century monk who carried out the first experiments into inheritance. He discovered that characteristics were caused by something he called 'hereditary units'.

Grade 4-6

a) Name the organisms that Mendel studied.

....
[1]

b) What do we now call Mendel's 'hereditary units'?

☐ **A** chromosomes   ☐ **B** genes   ☐ **C** nucleotides   ☐ **D** nuclei

[1]

c) Give **two** conclusions Mendel reached about hereditary units.

1. ....

....

2. ....

....
[2]

[Total 4 marks]

2 A gardener crosses pea plants that produce wrinkly seeds with pea plants that produce round seeds. All the offspring produce round seeds. She then crosses the offspring with each other. The results of the gardener's second cross are shown in **Figure 1**.

Grade 6-7

Figure 1

Number of plants with round seeds	Number of plants with wrinkly seeds
382	128

a) Calculate the ratio of offspring with round seeds to offspring with wrinkly seeds. Give your answer in its simplest form and to the nearest whole numbers.

ratio of round seeds : wrinkly seeds ....
[1]

b) Give **one** conclusion that can be made about the inheritance of round and wrinkly seeds from the gardener's experiment.

....

....
[1]

[Total 2 marks]

Genetic Diagrams

Warm-Up

Draw lines to match the words on the left to the correct definition on the right.

genotype   Having two alleles the same for a particular gene.

phenotype   The combination of alleles an organism has.

allele   The characteristics an organism has.

heterozygous   Having two different alleles for a particular gene.

homozygous   A version of a gene.

1   Height in pea plants is controlled by a single gene. The allele for tall plants (T) is dominant over the allele for dwarf plants (t). *Grade 4-6*

A student says that a pea plant must have the genotype TT to be tall.
Is the student correct? Explain your answer.

....

....

[Total 2 marks]

2   Polled cattle have no horns. The polled allele (N) is dominant over the allele for horns (n). A farmer wants to breed a herd of polled cattle. *Grade 6-7*

a) The farmer breeds a polled bull with a horned cow. Both the bull and the cow are homozygous for their trait.

Complete the Punnett square on the right to show the genotypes of the offspring.

	....	....
....	....	....
....	....	....

[1]

b) The farmer later breeds a heterozygous polled bull with several heterozygous polled cows. Give the likely ratio of polled cattle : horned cattle in the calves. Draw a genetic diagram to explain your answer.

ratio of polled calves : horned calves ....

[2]

[Total 3 marks]

Topic 3 — Genetics

3 **Figure 1** shows a tabby cat. Tabby cats have a distinctive banding pattern on their fur. The banding is controlled by a single gene. The allele for banding (B) is dominant over the allele for solid colour fur (b).

Figure 1

a) State the **two** possible genotypes for the cat shown in **Figure 1**.

1. .... 2. ....

[2]

b) A heterozygous tabby cat breeds with a cat with solid-colour fur.

i) Draw a genetic diagram to show the probability of one of the offspring being a tabby.

probability of one of the offspring being a tabby: ....

[2]

ii) The heterozygous tabby and the cat with solid-colour fur have 6 kittens. State how many of these kittens are likely to be tabby.

....

[1]

[Total 5 marks]

4 Hair length in Syrian hamsters is controlled by a single gene. The allele for short hair (H) is dominant over the allele for long hair (h).

Explain how a breeder could determine the genotype of a short-haired hamster.

....

....

....

....

....

....

[Total 4 marks]

Exam Practice Tip

You've really got to learn all the scientific words related to this topic (dominant, recessive, homozygous, etc.). Not only could you be asked to define them in the exam, it's assumed you'll know what the terms mean when they're used in questions. It's hard to get the right answer if you don't know what the question's asking you, so get learning that vocab.

More Genetic Diagrams

1 **Figure 1** shows how the gender of offspring is determined.

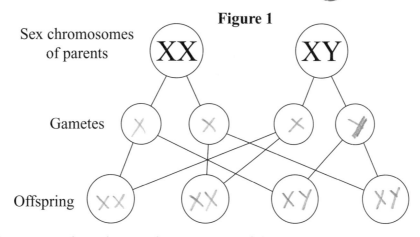

Figure 1

a) Complete **Figure 1** to show the sex chromosomes of the gametes and the offspring.

[1]

b) Give the ratio of male to female offspring. ....

[1]

[Total 2 marks]

2 PKU is a genetic disorder caused by a recessive allele (h). **Figure 2** shows a family pedigree for a family in which one of the children has PKU.

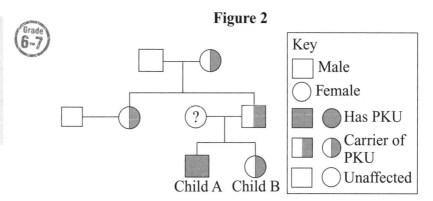

a) i) State the genotype of child A. ....

[1]

ii) State the **two** possible genotypes of Child A's mother.

1. .... 2. ....

[2]

b) Two carriers of PKU have a child. Complete the Punnett square to show the percentage probability that they will have a child who does **not** have the disorder.

probability of having a child who does not have the disorder: ....%

[2]

[Total 5 marks]

Sex-Linked Genetic Disorders

1 Red-green colour blindness is caused by a recessive allele (n) on the X chromosome. A man with red-green colour blindness has a child with a woman who is a carrier for the condition. **Figure 1** shows the possible genotypes of the couple's child.

Grade 6-7

Figure 1

	man	
	X^n	Y
woman X^N	$X^N X^n$	$X^N Y$
X^n	$X^n X^n$	$X^n Y$

a) Explain what it means if a person is a carrier of a genetic disorder.

....

....

....

[2]

b) Using **Figure 1**, state the probability that the couple will have:

i) a child with red-green colour blindness.

....

[1]

ii) a daughter with red-green colour blindness.

....

[1]

c) The couple have a boy. State the probability that the boy has red-green colour blindness.

....

[1]

[Total 5 marks]

2 Duchenne muscular dystrophy is a recessive X-linked disorder. About 1 in 3500 males is born with Duchenne muscular dystrophy compared to about 1 in 50 million females.

Grade 7-9

Suggest an explanation for the large difference in these two figures.

....

....

....

....

....

[Total 3 marks]

Topic 3 — Genetics

Inheritance of Blood Groups

Warm-Up

Are the following statements true or false? Circle the correct answer.

1) The allele for blood group O is recessive.   True / False
2) A person with blood group A must have the genotype I^AI^A.   True / False
3) Blood groups in humans are controlled by multiple genes.   True / False
4) A person whose parents are both blood group A can't be blood group O.   True / False

1 There are three alleles that control blood group in humans.

a) Blood group alleles I^A and I^B are codominant.
Explain what this means for the phenotype of a person with the genotype I^AI^B.

....

....
                                                                                    [2]

b) A man and a woman are both blood group B. They each have the genotype I^BI^O. The man and
the woman have a child together. Explain the possible blood groups their child could have.

....

....

....

....
                                                                                    [2]
                                                                          [Total 4 marks]

2 **Figure 1** shows the percentage of UK blood donors
with different blood groups.

a) What percentage of donors in **Figure 1**
definitely do **not** have the I^O allele?

                      ....%
                              [1]

b) Calculate the percentage of donors in
Figure 1 with the I^B allele.

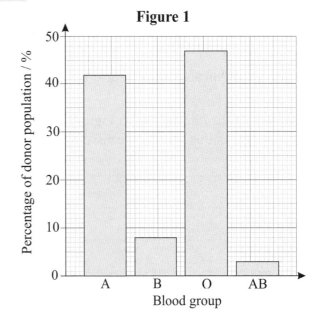

                      ....%
                              [2]
                      [Total 3 marks]

Variation

1   Mutations can have different effects on the phenotype of an organism.   (Grade 4-6)

a)   Explain what is meant by the term 'phenotype'.

....

[1]

b)   Which **one** of the following statements is true?

☐   **A**   A single mutation usually has a large effect on an organism's phenotype.

☐   **B**   Most mutations affect an organism's phenotype, but only slightly.

☐   **C**   Most mutations have no effect on an organism's phenotype.

☐   **D**   A single mutation never has any effect on an organism's phenotype.

[1]

[Total 2 marks]

2   An experiment was carried out into the causes of variation in plant height. Three different controlled environments (A, B and C) were set up. Five plants of the same species were grown from seed in each environment. The heights of all the plants were measured after six weeks and are shown in **Figure 1**.   (Grade 6-7)

Figure 1

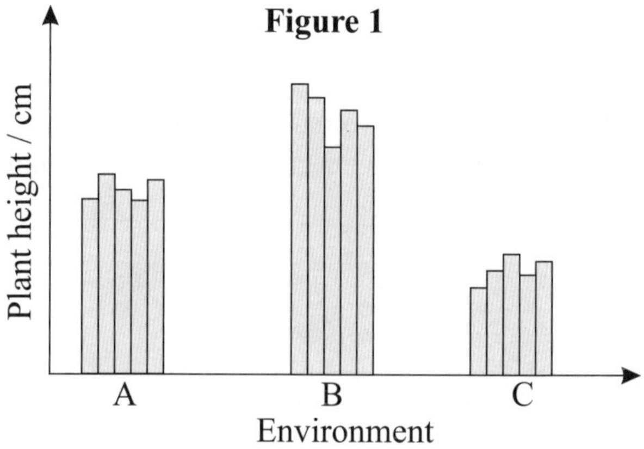

a)   Some variation in plants is genetic and can be caused by mutations. Give **one** other cause of genetic variation within a plant species.

....

[1]

b)   Some variation in plants can be caused by the environment. What name is given to a characteristic caused by environmental variation?

☐   **A**   an assisted characteristic   ☐   **C**   an additional characteristic

☐   **B**   an acquired characteristic   ☐   **D**   an advanced characteristic

[1]

c)   Using the information in **Figure 1**, explain whether variation in plant height in this species is caused by genes, the environment or both.

....

....

....

....

[4]

[Total 6 marks]

3   The heterozygosity index (H) can be used to measure the genetic variation
in a population. H always has a value between 0 and 1. The closer the
value to 1, the more alleles there are in the population. **Figure 2** shows
the value of H for three different populations of the same species in two
different years. The populations reproduce via sexual reproduction.

Figure 2

	Population 1	Population 2	Population 3
Value of H in 2005	0.42	0.41	0.48
Value of H in 2015	0.43	0.40	0.52

a) Calculate the difference in the mean value of H for the three populations,
between 2005 and 2015.

Difference in mean value: ....

[3]

b) Give **three** observations that can be made about the genetic variation
of these three populations from the data in **Figure 2**.

1. ....

....

2. ....

....

3. ....

....

[3]

c) Would you expect the population of an organism that only reproduces via asexual reproduction to
have a higher or lower value of H than the populations shown in **Figure 2**? Explain your answer.

....

....

....

....

[2]

[Total 8 marks]

Topic 3 — Genetics

The Human Genome Project

1 Scientists hope to be able to use knowledge gained from the Human Genome Project to improve the treatment of disease. *(Grade 6-7)*

a) Outline the aim of the Human Genome Project.

....

....

[1]

b) Describe **one** way in which knowledge gained from the Human Genome Project and related research could help scientists to develop new and better medicines.

....

....

[1]

c) Explain **one** way in which the Human Genome Project has affected the testing or treatment of inherited disorders.

....

....

....

....

[2]

[Total 4 marks]

2 Some genetic variants have been discovered that are associated with an increased risk of developing late onset Alzheimer's disease. However, there are currently no medically approved genetic tests for these variants. *(Grade 6-7)*

a) Explain **one** possible benefit of testing a person for genetic variants that are associated with an increased risk of developing Alzheimer's disease later in life.

....

....

....

[2]

b) Give **two** possible drawbacks of testing a person for these genetic variants.

1. ....

....

2. ....

....

[2]

[Total 4 marks]

Natural Selection and Evidence for Evolution

Fill in the blanks in the paragraph below using some of the words on the right.

predation
beneficial
survival
competition
offspring
used to
adapted to
stronger

Natural selection describes how .... alleles become more

common in a population. Selection pressures such as .... and

.... mean that not all organisms will survive and reproduce.

Individuals with alleles that make them better .... their environment

are more likely to survive and pass on their alleles to their ....

---

1   Organisms can only adapt to their environment
if there is genetic variation in the population.   Grade 4-6

a)   Individuals in a population show genetic variation because of differences in their:

☐   **A** selection pressures   ☐   **C** cells

☐   **B** alleles   ☐   **D** adaptations

[1]

b)   How do new alleles arise in a population of organisms?

....

[1]

[Total 2 marks]

---

2   Bacteria can quickly evolve resistance to a particular antibiotic.   Grade 6-7

a)   Suggest **one** reason why bacteria can evolve quickly.

....

[1]

b)   Explain how a bacterium could become less affected by a particular antibiotic.

....

[1]

c)   i)   State the selection pressure involved when bacteria develop resistance to an antibiotic.

....

[1]

ii)   Explain how antibiotic resistance becomes more common in a population over time.

....

....

....

[3]

[Total 6 marks]

3 Warfarin™ is an anti-blood-clotting drug. It can be used as a poison to kill rats. Some rat populations have evolved to become resistant to Warfarin.

(Grade 7-9)

a) Explain **one** benefit to the rats of developing resistance to Warfarin.

....

....

[2]

b) **Figure 1** shows how the percentage of Warfarin-resistant rats in a population changed after the introduction of Warfarin as a rat poison. Explain how this data provides evidence for evolution.

....

....

....

....

....

....

....

....

[4]

[Total 6 marks]

Figure 1

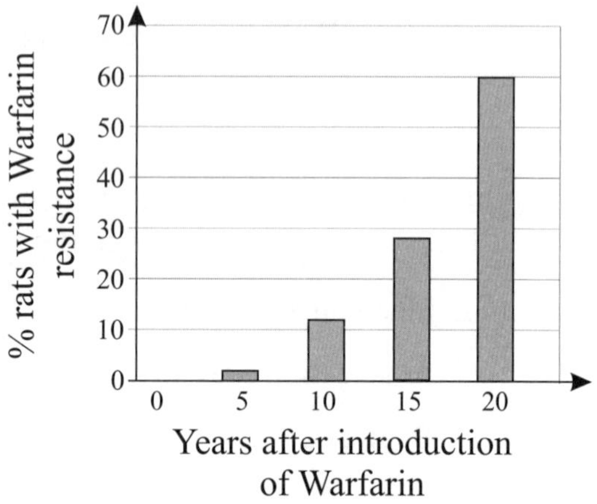

% rats with Warfarin resistance

Years after introduction of Warfarin

4* A population of finches on an island mainly eat seeds. The finches vary in the size of their beaks. Larger beaks are better for breaking apart larger seeds, whereas smaller beaks are better for picking up and eating smaller seeds. A storm kills off many of the plants that produce larger seeds.

(Grade 7-9)

Describe how evolution by natural selection may lead to a change in the beak size in the population of finches, following the storm.

....

....

....

....

....

....

....

....

[Total 6 marks]

Exam Practice Tip

Natural selection is a big favourite with examiners, so make sure you learn it well. If you get asked about natural selection in a context you haven't heard of before, don't panic — the process always involves the same steps in the same order. You just need to apply what you know to the information you're given in the question.

Darwin and Wallace

1 Alfred Russel Wallace and Charles Darwin both proposed theories about the evolution of organisms by natural selection.

Grade 6-7

a) What was the title of the book in which Charles Darwin proposed his theory of evolution by natural selection?

☐ **A** On the Theory of Evolution

☐ **B** On the Origin of Species

☐ **C** On the Process of Natural Selection

☐ **D** On the Progression of Organisms

[1]

b) Darwin's theory was based on observations he made whilst travelling around the world. Describe **two** observations Darwin made, upon which he based his theory.

1. ....

....

2. ....

....

[2]

c) Wallace's observations also provided evidence to support the theory of evolution by natural selection. Describe **one** piece of evidence Wallace found and explain how it supports the theory of evolution by natural selection.

....

....

....

[2]

[Total 5 marks]

2 The theory of evolution by natural selection is still important today.

Grade 6-7

Explain **two** ways in which modern biology has been affected by this theory.

1. ....

....

2. ....

....

[Total 2 marks]

Fossil Evidence for Human Evolution

Show the age of the fossils on the right by putting the correct name into each of the boxes on the timeline below.

'Lucy'   'Ardi'

'Turkana Boy'

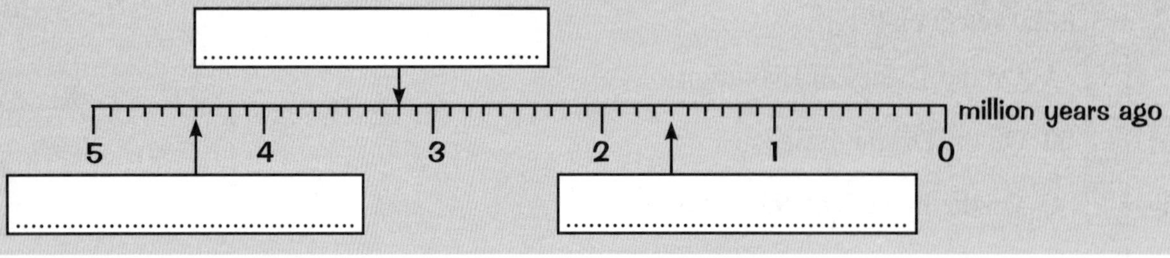

....

5   4   3   2   1   0   million years ago

....

---

1   'Turkana Boy' is a fossil of the species *Homo erectus*.   Grade 4-6

a) 'Turkana Boy' was discovered by the scientist:

☐ **A** Carl Woese   ☐ **C** Alfred Russel Wallace

☐ **B** Charles Darwin   ☐ **D** Richard Leakey

[1]

b) Give **two** features of the 'Turkana Boy' skeleton, which suggest that his species was more human-like than the species of 'Ardi' or 'Lucy'.

1. ....

2. ....

[2]

[Total 3 marks]

---

2   An anthropologist is comparing a number of skeletons of human ancestors. He estimates their brain sizes using their skull remains. His results are shown in **Figure 1**. **Figure 2** shows a timeline for the evolutionary history of some human ancestor species.   Grade 6-7

Figure 1

Specimen	1	2	3
Brain size (cm³)	950	325	457

Figure 2

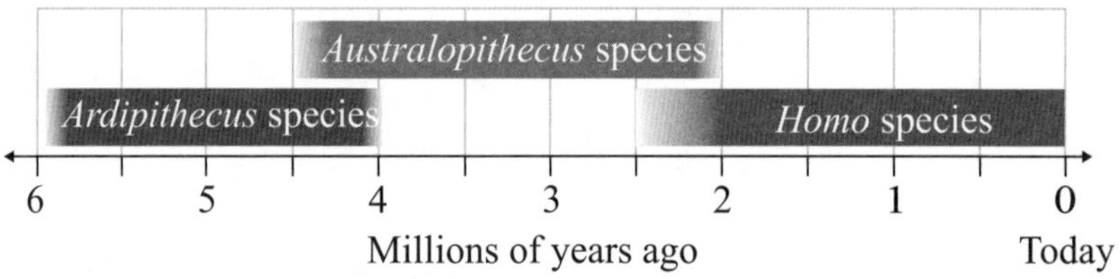

Australopithecus species

Ardipithecus species   *Homo* species

6   5   4   3   2   1   0

Millions of years ago   Today

a) Use **Figures 1** and **2** to determine which specimen (1, 2 or 3) is:

i) a *Homo* species ....

ii) an *Australopithecus* species ....

iii) an *Ardipithecus* species ....

[2]

b) Evidence suggests that species from further back in **Figure 2** were generally shorter in height than the more recent species. Suggest a physical reason for this.

....

[1]

[Total 3 marks]

3 Hominids are humans and their ancestors. Fossil hominids provide evidence for the evolutionary relationship between humans and apes.

Grade 7-9

Figure 3 shows the bone structure of a chimpanzee foot. Chimpanzees are apes. It also shows the foot bones of two incomplete fossil hominids and the bone structure of a human foot. Fossil A is older than fossil B.

Figure 3

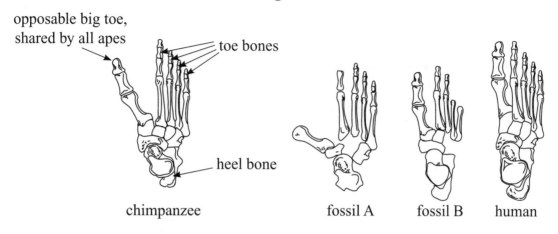

a) i) Using **Figure 3**, give **one** feature shared by **fossil A** and the chimpanzee, which is not found in humans.

....

[1]

ii) Suggest an explanation for why this feature is not found in humans.

....

....

[2]

b) How do the hominid fossils in **Figure 3** provide evidence for a shared common ancestor between humans and chimpanzees?

....

....

[1]

c) **Fossil B** belongs to the same species as the fossil 'Lucy'.
Other than differences in the foot structure, describe **one** difference you would expect to find between fossil B's skeleton and a chimpanzee's skeleton.

....

....

[1]

[Total 5 marks]

Exam Practice Tip

Make sure you know how features in our hominid ancestors changed over the course of evolutionary history. As hominids evolved to be more like humans and less like apes, legs became longer, arms became shorter and brains increased in size. Feet also become more adapted to walking than climbing trees.

Topic 4 — Natural Selection and Genetic Modification

More Evidence for Evolution

1 Humans and whales are both types of mammals.
They share several features, including a pentadactyl limb.   Grade 4-6

   a) Explain what is meant by the term 'pentadactyl limb'.

   ....

   [1]

   b) Explain how the presence of a pentadactyl limb in both
      humans and whales provides evidence for evolution.

   ....

   ....

   [1]

   [Total 2 marks]

2 Human ancestors began using stone tools around 2.6 million years ago.
Being able to date stone tools allows scientists to see how they developed over time.   Grade 6-7

Figure 1

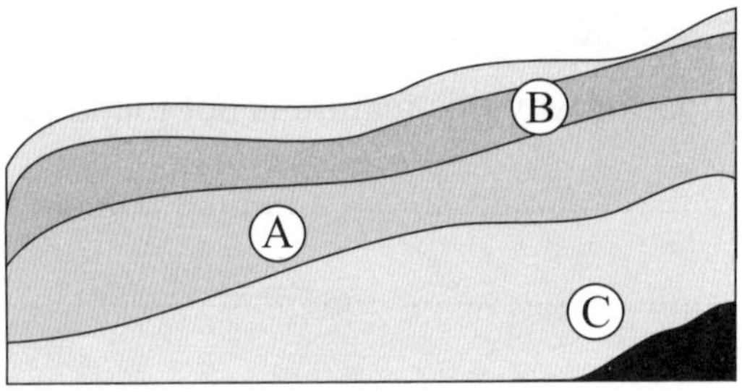

   a) i) **Figure 1** shows the distribution of three stone tools (A-C) across the layers of rock at a
         fossil site. Put the stone tools in most likely order of age, from oldest to youngest.

   ....

   [1]

   ii) Apart from studying the layers of rock that the tools are found in, give **two** methods that a
       scientist could use to date the stone tools at this fossil site.

   1. ....

   2. ....

   [2]

   b) Explain how stone tools provide evidence for the evolution of the brain in human ancestors.

   ....

   ....

   ....

   [2]

   [Total 5 marks]

Topic 4 — Natural Selection and Genetic Modification

Classification

1 Classification involves arranging living organisms into groups. In one system of classification, organisms are first arranged into five groups called kingdoms. Grade 4-6

a) Write down the five kingdoms in this classification system.

....

[1]

b) What is the correct order of the following groups in the five kingdom classification system, from biggest to smallest?

☐ **A** kingdom, phylum, class, order, family, species, genus

☐ **B** kingdom, family, order, class, phylum, species, genus

☐ **C** kingdom, phylum, genus, species, class, family, order

☐ **D** kingdom, phylum, class, order, family, genus, species

[1]

[Total 2 marks]

2 Nowadays, the three domain classification system is widely used to classify organisms. One of the domains is Eukarya. Grade 4-6

a) Fungi are part of the Eukarya domain.
State **three** other types of organism in the Eukarya domain.

....

[1]

b) Name the other **two** domains in the three domain system.

....

[2]

[Total 3 marks]

3 Changes in technology and chemical analyses led to the development of the three domain classification system in 1977. Grade 6-7

a) Explain how DNA sequencing techniques can be used to determine relationships between organisms.

....

....

....

[2]

b) Explain how RNA sequencing led to the prokaryote kingdom being split into two domains.

....

....

....

[2]

[Total 4 marks]

Topic 4 — Natural Selection and Genetic Modification

Selective Breeding

1 Selective breeding can be used to produce organisms with characteristics that are useful to humans. Grade 4-6

   a) Suggest **two** uses of selective breeding in agriculture.

     1. ....

     2. ....

[2]

   b) Suggest **one** use of selective breeding in medical research.

     ....

[1]

[Total 3 marks]

2 A farmer discovers that some of his dairy cows produce a little more milk per day than the rest of his herd. Grade 7-9

   a) Explain the steps that the farmer could take to breed a herd of cows with high milk yields from his existing herd.

     ....

     ....

     ....

     ....

     ....

[3]

   b) Weaver Syndrome is a genetic defect found in dairy cows. After successfully breeding cows with high milk yields, the farmer notices that more of his cows have Weaver Syndrome than in his previous herd. Suggest a reason for this.

     ....

     ....

     ....

[2]

   c) Explain why the emergence of an infectious disease, such as bovine tuberculosis, may be more of an issue for the farmer's new herd than for his previous herd.

     ....

     ....

     ....

     ....

[3]

[Total 8 marks]

Topic 4 — Natural Selection and Genetic Modification

Tissue Culture

1 Plants can be cloned in large numbers using tissue culture. Grade 4-6

   a) What does it mean if two individual plants are clones of each other?

     ....

     [1]

   b) Give **two** advantages of using tissue culture to grow clones of a single plant.

     1. ....

     2. ....

     [2]

   c) Which of these parts of a plant is most useful for producing a tissue culture?

     ☐ **A** leaf

     ☐ **B** flower

     ☐ **C** shoot tip

     ☐ **D** seed

     [1]

     [Total 4 marks]

2 Before being used to treat patients, all drugs go through rigorous tests. Some of these tests are done on animal tissue cultures. Grade 6-7

   a) Explain why animal tissue cultures are useful for testing the effects of drugs.

     ....

     ....

     ....

     [1]

   b) Describe how you could produce a tissue culture of rat liver cells for drug testing.

     ....

     ....

     ....

     ....

     ....

     ....

     ....

     [4]

     [Total 5 marks]

        Topic 4 — Natural Selection and Genetic Modification

Genetic Engineering

Warm-Up

Draw lines to connect each word or phrase on the
left with the statement describing it on the right.

restriction enzyme	a type of vector
plasmid	cuts DNA open
ligase	an organism with DNA from a different species
GM organism	sticks DNA ends together
vector	transfers DNA into a cell

1   Genetic engineering involves modifying the genome of one   Grade 6-7
     organism by introducing a gene from another organism.

   a) i) Outline how a desired gene would be isolated from an organism.

   ....

   ....
                                                                                                                    [1]

   ii) Explain how a vector can be used to insert the gene into a bacterial cell.

   ....

   ....

   ....

   ....
                                                                                                                    [3]

   b) Which of these is an example of a vector used in genetic engineering?

   ☐ **A** a hybridoma

   ☐ **B** a virus

   ☐ **C** a glucose molecule

   ☐ **D** a protein
                                                                                                                    [1]

   c) Explain **one** advantage of being able to insert the gene for a desired protein into a bacterial cell.

   ....

   ....
                                                                                                                    [2]
                                                                                                        [Total 7 marks]

2 Genetically modified corn plants are grown in many parts of the world due to their pest resistance.

Grade 6-7

a) Apart from pest resistance, give another example of a beneficial characteristic that could be introduced into a crop by genetic modification.

....
[1]

b) Give **two** reasons why some people may have concerns about the use of genetically modified crops in agriculture.

1. ....

....

2. ....

....
[2]

[Total 3 marks]

3* A scientist discovers that she is able to genetically modify hens to produce particular proteins in the whites of their eggs.

Grade 7-9

Discuss the potential advantages of the scientist's findings in medicine and other areas, and also the concerns that some people may have over genetically engineering animals.

....

....

....

....

....

....

....

....

....

....

....

[Total 6 marks]

Exam Practice Tip

Make sure you know plenty of arguments both for and against genetic engineering — they're the sort of thing examiners love to ask about. And don't forget the basic principles of using vectors and enzymes to genetically modify an organism — the techniques may vary a little depending on whether it's an animal/plant etc., but the basic idea is still the same.

Topic 4 — Natural Selection and Genetic Modification

GMOs and Human Population Growth

1   Genetically engineering crops to be pest-resistant increases
the yield of crops by decreasing the damage done by pests.

Grade 6-7

a) Explain how the bacterium *Bacillus thuringiensis* can be used
to introduce pest resistance into a crop.

....

....

....

....

....

[3]

b) Give **two** reasons why some people may be concerned about
using this method to make crops resistant to pests.

1. ....

....

2. ....

....

[2]

[Total 5 marks]

2   It is predicted that the worldwide population will reach 11 billion
people by 2100. Climate change may also lead to drought and pest
problems in many regions in 2100, affecting our ability to grow food.

Grade 6-7

a) Explain how genetically modified crops may be helpful for a population
in a drought-affected region in 2100.

....

....

....

[3]

One method for controlling pest problems in the future is to develop new chemical pesticides.
Another is to use biological control methods.

b) Give **one** advantage and **one** disadvantage of using biological control methods to control pests
instead of chemical pesticides.

Advantage ....

Disadvantage ....

[2]

[Total 5 marks]

Topic 4 — Natural Selection and Genetic Modification

Health and Disease

Warm-Up

Write the type of pathogen that causes each of the diseases below, using the words on the right. You may use a word more than once.

Chalara ash dieback	....	protist
Ebola	....	virus
Tuberculosis	....	fungus
Malaria	....	
Cholera	....	bacterium

1   The World Health Organisation (WHO) monitors the health of people worldwide and coordinates research into communicable and non-communicable diseases.   *Grade 4-6*

a) Give the WHO's definition of health.

....

....

[2]

b) Describe the difference between a communicable and a non-communicable disease.

....

....

[1]

[Total 3 marks]

2   Stomach ulcers can be caused by a pathogen.   *Grade 4-6*

a) Which of the following is the name of the pathogen that can cause stomach ulcers?

☐ **A** *Vibrio cholerae*   ☐ **C** *Helicobacter pylori*

☐ **B** *Mycobacterium tuberculosis*   ☐ **D** *Enterococcus faecalis*

[1]

b) i) Explain why the spread of the pathogen in developing countries may be prevented by the building of good drainage systems.

....

....

....

[2]

ii) Name **one** other disease which may be prevented from spreading by the building of good drainage systems in developing countries.

....

[1]

[Total 4 marks]

3 Chalara ash dieback disease was originally noticed in ash trees in Poland in the 1990s. In 2012, a case of ash dieback was diagnosed in Britain, and it is now very widespread.

Grade 6-7

a) Give **two** symptoms of chalara ash dieback disease.

....

[2]

b) Suggest **one** way in which the disease may have been transmitted from Poland to Britain.

....

[1]

c) Describe **one** precaution that could be taken to limit any further spread of the disease.

....

....

[1]

[Total 4 marks]

4* Malaria is caused by a microorganism called *Plasmodium*. *Plasmodium* can only cause malaria if it is able to complete its growth cycle, which can only happen if temperatures are high enough. In many countries affected by malaria, climate change is leading to an increase in temperature at higher altitudes, where malaria was not previously present.

Grade 7-9

Explain why it may be advisable for people in high altitude areas of countries affected by malaria to learn how to use mosquito nets.

....

....

....

....

....

....

....

....

....

....

....

....

....

[Total 6 marks]

Exam Practice Tip

There are a lot of communicable diseases that you need to know about for the exam. Make sure you know the pathogen that causes each one, the effects it causes, how it is spread and how its transmission can be prevented. Take the time to learn them all properly — if you get them mixed up in the exam you could be throwing away marks.

Topic 5 — Health, Disease and the Development of Medicines

Viruses and STIs

1 *Chlamydia* is a disease which may result in infertility. (Grade 4-6)

a) Name the type of pathogen that causes *Chlamydia*.

....

[1]

b) State how *Chlamydia* is most commonly transmitted between individuals.

....

[1]

c) Give **one** method for preventing the spread of *Chlamydia*.

....

[1]

[Total 3 marks]

2 HIV is a virus that eventually leads to AIDS in the people it infects. (Grade 6-7)
After entering cells, HIV enters the lysogenic stage of its life cycle.

a) After the initial period of infection a person may be symptomless for a very long time.
Explain why this is the case.

....

....

....

[2]

b) Explain why a person with AIDS may become seriously ill due to infection by another pathogen.

....

....

....

[2]

c) Suggest an explanation as to why, in order to protect themselves from HIV,
drug users should not share needles.

....

....

....

[2]

[Total 6 marks]

Topic 5 — Health, Disease and the Development of Medicines

3 All viruses have a lytic stage in their life cycle. **Grade 6-7**

a) Describe the lytic pathway in the life cycle of a virus from the moment the virus attaches itself onto the surface of a host cell.

....

....

....

....

....

[4]

b) Explain why viruses are dependent on living cells in order to reproduce.

....

....

[1]

[Total 5 marks]

4 Sequencing techniques allow scientists to read all of the DNA in an organism. A group of scientists infect a sample of *Helicobacter pylori* cells with a virus and then sequence the genome of some of the cells in the sample. They notice viral DNA alongside bacterial DNA in the genome sequence. **Grade 7-9**

a) From their findings, give **one** conclusion about the life cycle of the virus infecting the bacteria.

....

[1]

b) The scientists exposed the sample of bacteria used for DNA sequencing to UV radiation. Suggest an explanation as to why this caused many of the cells in the sample to burst.

....

....

....

....

....

....

[4]

[Total 5 marks]

> **Exam Practice Tip**
>
> If you know loads about a particular topic don't be tempted to just write down everything you know and hope for the best. Take time to read the question carefully, make sure what you write down definitely answers the question and don't waste time writing too much, e.g. details of the lysogenic pathway when you've only been asked about the lytic pathway.

Topic 5 — Health, Disease and the Development of Medicines

Plant Diseases

1 Plants use a range of strategies to help to protect themselves from pests and pathogens. *(Grade 4-6)*

a) Explain **one** way in which a waxy cuticle on the surface of leaves protects a plant from pests or pathogens.

....

....

[1]

b) Explain **one** way in which plants use chemicals to protect themselves from pests or pathogens.

....

....

[1]

[Total 2 marks]

2 A plant pathologist notices that several plants he is studying have spots on their leaves. He decides to determine the cause of the spots. *(Grade 6-7)*

a) Suggest how the plant pathologist could determine whether or not the spots are caused by a nutrient deficiency in the plant.

....

....

[2]

b) The plant pathologist finds that the spots are caused by a pathogen. Explain why the distribution of the infected plants may help to determine the type of pathogen involved.

....

....

....

[1]

c) He suspects that the pathogen involved is a type of bacteria. He takes a sample of the infected plant tissue and performs a diagnostic test to determine the pathogen involved. Describe what he may have added to the infected plant tissue sample in the diagnostic test.

....

....

[1]

[Total 4 marks]

   Topic 5 — Health, Disease and the Development of Medicines

Fighting Disease

1 The body has many features which it can use to protect itself against pathogens. **Grade 4-6**

a) Give **one** example of a physical barrier against pathogens in humans.

....

[1]

b) What is the name of the enzyme present in tears which kills bacteria on the surface of the eye?

☐ **A** carbohydrase   ☐ **B** protease   ☐ **C** amylase   ☐ **D** lysozyme

[1]

c) Name the chemical which kills most pathogens that reach the stomach.

....

[1]

[Total 3 marks]

2 B-lymphocytes are a type of white blood cell involved in the specific immune response. **Grade 6-7**

a) State what is meant by the term 'specific immune response'.

....

[1]

b) Explain how B-lymphocytes help the body to fight against invading pathogens.

....

....

....

....

....

[4]

[Total 5 marks]

3 Primary cilia dyskinesia (PCD) is a disease in which cilia don't work properly. Suggest an explanation as to why people with PCD are likely to get frequent lung infections. **Grade 7-9**

....

....

....

....

....

[Total 3 marks]

Topic 5 — Health, Disease and the Development of Medicines

Memory Lymphocytes and Immunisation

1 Children are often immunised against measles. *Grade 4-6*

a) Which of the following processes is stimulated following immunisation?

☐ **A** Antibodies produce B-lymphocytes.   ☐ **C** Red blood cells produce antibodies.

☐ **B** B-lymphocytes produce antibiotics.   ☐ **D** B-lymphocytes produce antibodies.

[1]

b) Give **one** reason why some parents may choose not to have their children immunised.

....

[1]

c) Describe what it means if a person is 'immune' to a disease.

....

....

[1]

[Total 3 marks]

2 Antibodies are important proteins in the immune response to a pathogen. **Figure 1** shows how the concentration of a particular antibody in the blood of a person changes over time. *Grade 6-7*

Figure 1

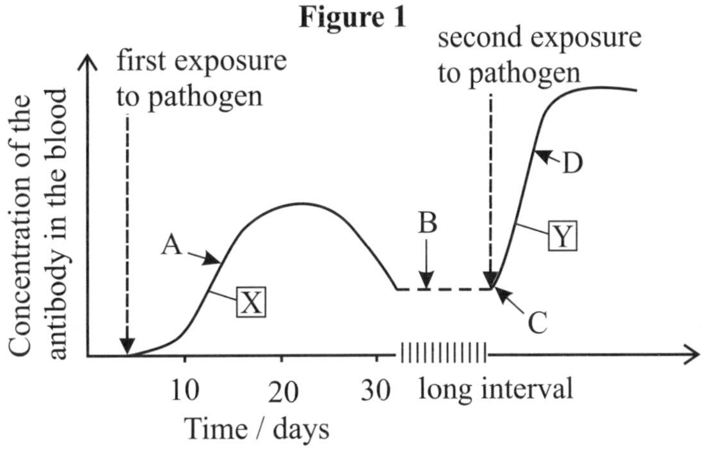

a) At which point on the graph (**A**, **B**, **C** or **D**) are memory lymphocytes first produced?

☐ **A**   ☐ **B**   ☐ **C**   ☐ **D**

[1]

b) Explain why the curve on **Figure 1** labelled **Y** is steeper than the curve labelled **X**.

....

....

....

....

[3]

[Total 4 marks]

Topic 5 — Health, Disease and the Development of Medicines

3 When visiting some other countries, it is recommended that travellers are vaccinated against some of the serious diseases found in the country. **(Grade 6-7)**

a) If a traveller planned to visit a country where there had been a recent outbreak of the communicable disease cholera, they might get vaccinated against cholera before they travelled. Give **two** reasons why this would be beneficial.

1. ....

2. ....

[2]

b) Some countries insist that travellers have had particular vaccinations before they are allowed to enter the country. Suggest why.

....

....

[1]

[Total 3 marks]

4 In 1988 the World Health Organisation began a global immunisation programme to try to eradicate polio. By 2014, incidence of polio had been reduced by 99.9%. **(Grade 7-9)**

a) Before being used in immunisation, the virus which causes polio is first treated with a chemical called formaldehyde. Suggest a reason for this.

....

[1]

b) Explain why a person who has been immunised against polio would be less likely to develop the disease if the virus entered their body.

....

....

....

....

....

[3]

c) Sometimes it isn't possible to immunise people with weakened immune systems. Explain why global immunisation programmes can still protect these people from a disease even if they aren't immunised themselves.

....

....

....

....

....

[2]

[Total 6 marks]

Topic 5 — Health, Disease and the Development of Medicines

Monoclonal Antibodies

Circle the correct underlined words below so that each sentence is correct.

Monoclonal antibodies are made using <u>lymphocytes</u>/<u>erythrocytes</u>. They can be used to locate particular pathogens in a blood sample by being bound to a fluorescent <u>dye</u>/<u>antigen</u>. The monoclonal antibodies will <u>attach to</u>/<u>kill</u> the pathogen and can be detected.

1 Monoclonal antibodies are engineered by scientists. *(Grade 6-7)*

a) Monoclonal antibodies are:

☐ **A** identical to each other and specific to one type of antigen.

☐ **B** different to each other and will bind to different types of antigen.

☐ **C** identical to each other and will bind to different types of antigen.

☐ **D** different to each other and specific to one type of antigen.

[1]

b) During the production of monoclonal antibodies, scientists use antibody-producing cells from animals such as mice. Explain why they must first inject the animal with an antigen.

....

....

....

[2]

c) During the next stage of monoclonal antibody production, an antibody-producing cell and a tumour cell are fused to produce a new type of cell.

i) What is the name of the new type of cell produced?

☐ **A** carcinoma cell   ☐ **C** hybridoma cell

☐ **B** melanoma cell   ☐ **D** myeloma cell

[1]

ii) Explain why a tumour cell is used to produce the new type of cell.

....

....

....

....

[3]

[Total 7 marks]

2   During pregnancy a woman begins to produce hCG hormone, which becomes present in her urine. **Figure 1** shows a pregnancy test that uses monoclonal antibodies to detect this hormone.

Figure 1

Blue beads with antibodies attached.

Antibody attached to strip.

Test strip

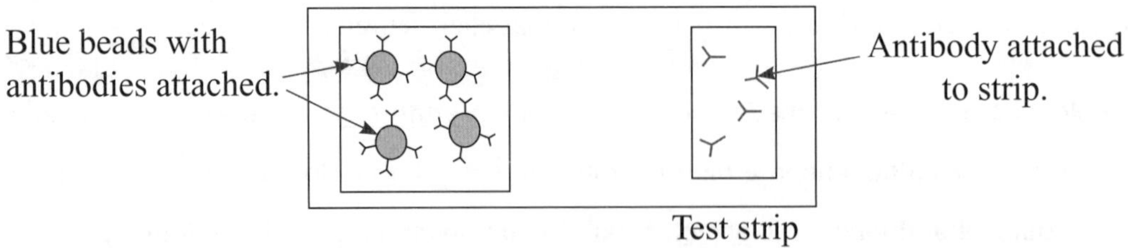

Explain how this test can show if the hCG hormone is present in a woman's urine.

....

....

....

....

....

....

[Total 4 marks]

3   Monoclonal antibodies have many medical applications, including in the treatment of cancer and the detection of blood clots.

a) Explain why it is advantageous to use monoclonal antibodies over other forms of cancer treatment, such as normal drug and radiotherapy treatments.

....

....

....

....

[3]

b) Explain how radioactively-labelled monoclonal antibodies can be used to visualise blood clots.

....

....

....

....

....

....

[3]

[Total 6 marks]

Antibiotics and Other Medicines

1   New drugs have to undergo pre-clinical and clinical testing before they can be used.   (Grade 4-6)

   a)   i)   Preclinical testing is carried out on:

☐   **A**   healthy human volunteers   ☐   **C**   patients in a hospital

☐   **B**   human cells, tissues and dead animals   ☐   **D**   human cells, tissues and live animals

[1]

     ii)   Give **one** thing which is investigated during the pre-clinical testing of drugs.

....

[1]

   b)   Suggest why very low doses of the drug are given at the start of clinical trials.

....

[1]

   c)   Placebos and double-blind methods are often used in clinical trials.

     i)   Explain why placebos are used.

....

....

[1]

     ii)   Explain why double-blind trials are used.

....

....

[1]

[Total 5 marks]

2   Antibiotics are used to cure many different diseases.   (Grade 6-7)

   a)   Explain why antibiotics can be used to treat bacterial pathogens in humans.

....

....

[2]

   b)   Antibiotics are not effective against viruses.
      Suggest an explanation as to why it is difficult to develop drugs that target viral pathogens.

....

....

....

[2]

[Total 4 marks]

Investigating Antibiotics and Antiseptics

1   **Figure 1** shows the effect of two different antibiotics (labelled **A** and **B**) on two different cultures of the bacteria *Staphylococcus aureus* (labelled **culture 1** and **2**).

Grade 6-7

Figure 1

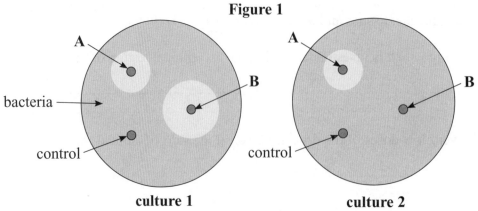

culture 1   culture 2

a) The clear zones on the plate are called zones of:

   ☐   **A**   inhibition   ☐   **B**   exhibition   ☐   **C**   resistance   ☐   **D**   bacterial growth

[1]

b) Use **Figure 1** to calculate the area of the clear zone around antibiotic **B** in **culture 1**. Give your answer to 3 significant figures.

$\pi = 3.14$

area of clear zone = ...mm^2

[3]

c) Suggest an explanation for the lack of a clear zone around antibiotic **B** in **culture 2**.

....

....

[2]

d) **Culture 1** was spread on four different agar plates and retested with antibiotic **A**. The size of the clear zones around the antibiotic on each plate are shown in **Figure 2**.

Figure 2

Plate	1	2	3	4
Area of clear zone (mm^2)	85	76	12	80

   i) Calculate the mean size of the clear zone around antibiotic **A** for all four plates.

mean size of clear zone = ... mm^2

[2]

   ii) Suggest an explanation for the result on plate 3.

....

[1]

[Total 9 marks]

2 An investigation is carried out to examine the effects of different antiseptics on a species of bacteria. A solution of agar is prepared and poured into a Petri dish. It is then left uncovered to dry.

Grade 6-7 **PRACTICAL**

a) Once the agar is dry the plate is examined and found to be contaminated.
There are several small bacterial colonies on the agar plate, as illustrated in **Figure 3**.
Calculate the area of colony **A** in **Figure 3**.
Give your answer to 2 significant figures.

$\pi = 3.14$

Figure 3

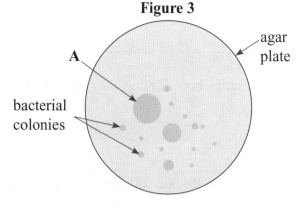

agar plate

A

bacterial colonies

Area of colony A = ...mm^2

[3]

b) A different agar plate is prepared for the experiment. Give **two** aseptic techniques that should be used when preparing the new plate so that it doesn't become contaminated.

1. ....

2. ....

[2]

c) Once the new plate is ready, bacteria grown in a culture vial are spread over the surface of the agar using an inoculating loop. Give **two** aseptic techniques that should be used when spreading the bacteria.

1. ....

2. ....

[2]

d) **Figure 4** shows what the plate looked like after it had been incubated.
Explain why it might be difficult to test the effects of different antiseptics on this plate of bacteria.

Figure 4 agar plate

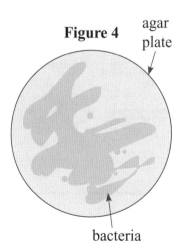

bacteria

....

....

....

....

[2]

[Total 9 marks]

Exam Practice Tip

When you're finding the area of a clear zone or of a bacterial colony, make sure that you're really careful with your measurements. Also make sure to write out all of your working — it'll be easier to check your work to see if you've made any silly mistakes and you might also pick up some marks for your working even if your final answer is wrong.

Non-Communicable Diseases

1   Non-communicable diseases are not spread by pathogens, instead they are associated with risk factors.   Grade 4-6

   a)   Describe what is meant by a 'risk factor' for a disease.

   ....

   ....
   [1]

   b)   Describe how drinking too much alcohol can cause liver disease.

   ....

   ....
   [2]

   c)   Give **one** disease which is associated with smoking.

   ....
   [1]

   [Total 4 marks]

2*   Being overweight or obese in childhood is an important risk factor for developing obesity as an adult. One of the main aims of the UK government's Change4Life campaign is to tackle childhood obesity.   Grade 7-9

   Explain which lifestyle factors Change4Life is likely to tackle and the economical reasons why the government may have developed this campaign.

   ....

   ....

   ....

   ....

   ....

   ....

   ....

   ....

   ....

   ....
   [Total 6 marks]

Exam Practice Tip

Think carefully about 6 mark questions like the one on this page. Don't just start scribbling everything you know about the topic. Stop and think first — work out what the question is wanting you to write about, and then make sure you write enough points to bag yourself as many marks as possible. Good job you've got some practice on this page...

Topic 5 — Health, Disease and the Development of Medicines

Measures of Obesity

1 A woman decides to lose weight by reducing her calorie intake. She is 170 cm tall and before she starts to reduce her calorie intake she has a mass of 73.5 kg. Her waist circumference is 91 cm and her hips circumference is 84 cm.

a) Calculate her waist-to-hip ratio.
Give your answer to 2 significant figures.

waist-to-hip ratio = ...
[1]

b) **Figure 1** shows weight descriptions for a range of BMI values.

Figure 1

i) Calculate her BMI before she starts to reduce her calorie intake. Give your answer to 3 significant figures.

Body Mass Index	Weight Description
below 18.5	underweight
18.5 - 24.9	normal
25 - 29.9	overweight
30 - 40	moderately obese
above 40	severely obese

BMI = ...kg m^{-2}
[3]

ii) After six months of her reduced calorie intake her BMI is calculated as 19. Using **Figure 1**, explain why her doctor advised her to consider increasing her calorie intake again.

....
[1]

[Total 5 marks]

2 Patients at a health centre had their BMI and waist-to-hip ratios calculated as part of a survey. The results of five of the patients are shown in **Figure 2**. A waist-to-hip ratio over 1 in men and over 0.85 in women indicates obesity.

a) Using **Figure 2**, explain which patient **(A-E)** is most at risk of developing cardiovascular disease.

....

....

....
[2]

Figure 2

Patient	Sex	BMI	Waist-to-hip ratio
A	Female	19.2	0.9
B	Male	26.1	0.9
C	Female	30.3	1.2
D	Female	30.5	0.7
E	Male	30.6	1.0

b) **Patient D** is a fitness instructor. Explain why her BMI may be misleading when assessing her risk of developing obesity-related disorders.

....

....

....
[2]

[Total 4 marks]

Treatments for Cardiovascular Disease

Use the correct words to fill in the gaps in the passage. Not all of them will be used.

asthma   cystic fibrosis   arteries

heart   lungs   respiration rate   veins   strokes   blood pressure

Cardiovascular disease is a term used to describe diseases of the blood vessels and

.... A high level of cholesterol in the blood and a high

.... can lead to cardiovascular disease by causing fatty

deposits to build up in .... This restricts blood flow,

which can lead to problems such as ....

1 Doctors were assessing the heart of a patient who had recently suffered from a heart attack. (Grade 6-7)
They noticed that one of the main arteries supplying the heart muscle was narrowed.

a) Give **two** pieces of lifestyle advice the doctors are likely to give to the patient.

1. ....

2. ....

[2]

b) The doctors tell the patient he could have a surgical procedure to reduce the chance of having
another heart attack.

i) Explain how a surgical procedure could improve the patient's condition.

....

....

[2]

ii) If the patient decides to go ahead with surgery, give **two** risks he should be made aware of.

1. ....

2. ....

[2]

c) Give **two** examples of medication that the patient could take to
improve his condition. Explain what each medication does.

1. ....

....

2. ....

....

[4]

[Total 10 marks]

Topic 5 — Health, Disease and the Development of Medicines

Photosynthesis

Complete the following passage using words on the right. You do not need to use all the words.

Photosynthesis is carried out by organisms such as green plants

and .... It uses energy transferred by

.... to produce ....

This energy is absorbed by subcellular structures called

....

mitochondria

glucose   algae

fungi   chloroplasts

minerals

fructose

light

---

1   Photosynthesis is a chemical reaction, which allows
    photosynthetic organisms to generate their own food source.   *Grade 4-6*

   a) Complete the word equation for photosynthesis.

      .... + ... → .... + ...

      [1]

   b) Photosynthesis is an endothermic reaction. This means that:

      ☐ **A** energy is taken in during the reaction.

      ☐ **B** energy is transferred to the surroundings during the reaction.

      ☐ **C** energy is made during the reaction.

      ☐ **D** energy is broken down during the reaction.

      [1]

      [Total 2 marks]

---

2   The sugar produced in photosynthesis can be broken
    down to transfer energy as part of respiration in a plant.   *Grade 6-7*

   a) Give **one** other way in which a plant uses the sugar produced by photosynthesis.

      ....

      [1]

   b) Explain why photosynthesis is important for the majority of life on Earth.

      ....

      ....

      ....

      ....

      [3]

      [Total 4 marks]

3 *Myriophyllum* is an aquatic plant. A student decided to investigate the effect of light intensity on the rate of photosynthesis in *Myriophyllum*.

The student set up a conical flask containing a solution of sodium hydrogencarbonate next to a lamp. She then took five *Myriophyllum* plants and placed them in the conical flask. Finally, she sealed and attached a gas syringe to the test tube and measured the amount of gas collected from the flask in two hours. She repeated this for four more flasks at different distances from the lamp. Her results are shown in **Figure 1**.

Figure 1

Conical flask	Distance away from light (cm)	Gas collected (cm³)	Rate of gas production (cm³ h⁻¹)
1	0	7.8	3.9
2	10	5.0	2.5
3	20	6.0	3.0
4	30	3.4	1.7
5	40	1.2	X

a) Name the gas collected in the gas syringe.

....

[1]

b) Calculate the rate of gas production in **Conical flask 5**.

X = ... cm³ h⁻¹

[1]

c) i) Using the results in **Figure 1**, describe and explain the effect of the distance from the lamp on the rate of gas production in *Myriophyllum*.

....

....

....

....

[3]

ii) Suggest **one** way in which you could increase your confidence in the answer you gave to part c) i).

....

[1]

d) Explain why it is important that the test tubes are all next to the same lamp.

....

....

[2]

[Total 8 marks]

Limiting Factors in Photosynthesis

1 The distance of a plant from a light source affects the plant's rate of photosynthesis. *(Grade 6-7)*

a) Name the mathematical law that governs the relationship between light intensity and distance from a light source.

....

[1]

b) A plant is 40 cm away from a light source. The plant is moved so that it is 20 cm away from the same light source. Describe how the intensity of light reaching the plant will change.

....

[1]

c) Describe how carbon dioxide concentration also affects the rate of photosynthesis.

....

....

[2]

[Total 4 marks]

2 **Figure 1** shows how temperature affects the rate of photosynthesis in a green plant. *(Grade 6-7)*

Figure 1

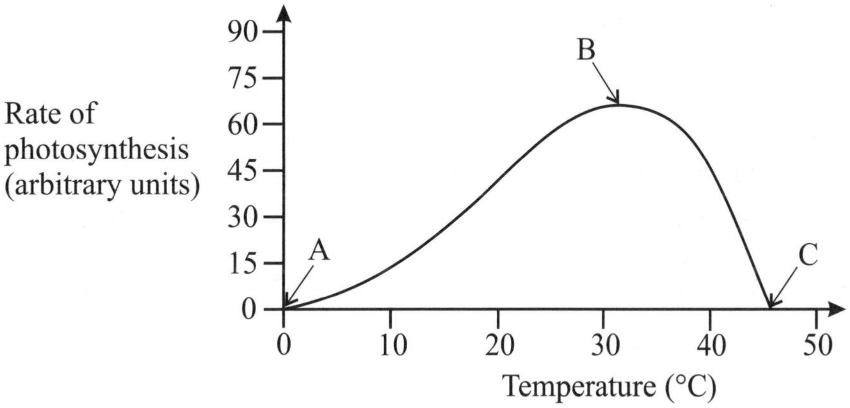

a) Describe and explain the shape of the curve in **Figure 1** between points **A** and **B**.

....

....

....

[2]

b) Describe and explain the shape of the curve between points **B** and **C**.

....

....

....

....

[3]

[Total 5 marks]

Topic 6 — Plant Structures and Their Functions

Transport in Plants

The diagrams below show two different types of vessel involved in the transport of substances in plants. Label them using the words on the right.

A. ....

B. ....

C. ....

D. Cell wall strengthened by

....

E. ....

F. ....

xylem tube

dead cells

living cells

end wall with pores

phloem tube

lignin

1   Xylem and phloem tubes are important vessels, which run the length of a plant.   Grade 4-6

a) i) Name **one** molecule transported via the phloem.

....

[1]

ii) Name **two** molecules transported via the xylem.

1. ....   2. ....

[2]

b) Transport via the phloem:

☐ **A** requires energy.   ☐ **C** only occurs in the leaves.

☐ **B** is called transpiration.   ☐ **D** only moves substances upwards from the roots.

[1]

[Total 4 marks]

2   *Pythium aphanidermatum* is a pathogen that can infect the roots of a plant, leading to the destruction of many of the root hair cells.   Grade 7-9

a) Explain how *Pythium* infection may disrupt the transpiration stream.

....

....

....

[2]

b) Why might plants infected with *Pythium* show signs of nutrient deficiency?

....

....

....

[2]

[Total 4 marks]

Topic 6 — Plant Structures and Their Functions

Stomata and Transpiration

1 Stomata are mostly found on the lower surface of leaves. **Grade 4-6**

a) State the main function of the stomata.

....
[1]

b) Name the cells which control the size of the stomata.

....
[1]

c) Explain how the stomata can affect the movement of water up the plant by transpiration.

....

....

....

....
[3]

[Total 5 marks]

2 A group of students were investigating the effect of air flow on the rate of transpiration. They set up their apparatus as shown in **Figure 1**. **Grade 6-7**

Figure 1

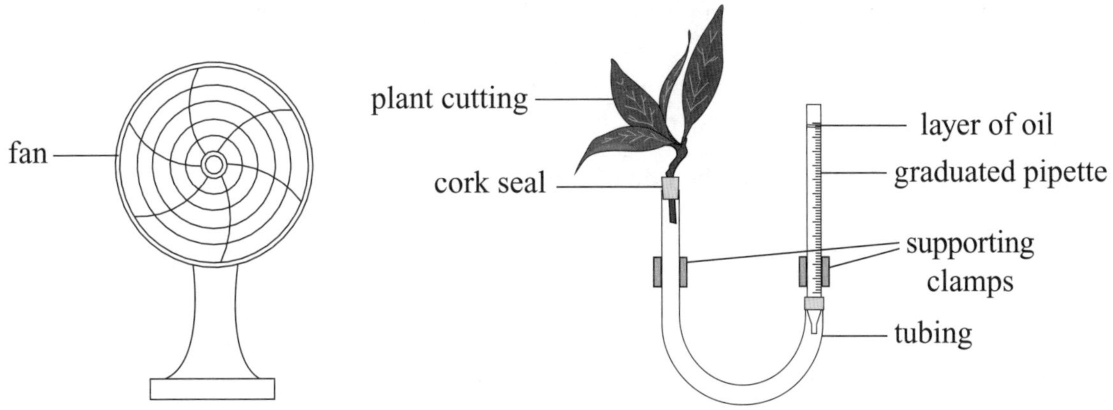

a) The tubing and graduated pipette were filled with water.
Suggest why a layer of oil was added to the surface of the water in the pipette.

....
[1]

The students recorded the change in the volume of water in the pipette over 30 minutes, in normal conditions. They repeated this five times. They then carried out these steps with the fan turned on to simulate windy conditions. **Figure 2** on the next page shows their results.

Figure 2

	Repeat	1	2	3	4	5	Mean
Water uptake in 30 minutes (cm^3)	Still Air	1.2	1.2	1.0	0.8	1.1	1.1
	Moving Air	2.0	1.8	2.3	1.9	1.7	1.9

b) Draw a bar chart to show the mean water uptake for still air and moving air.

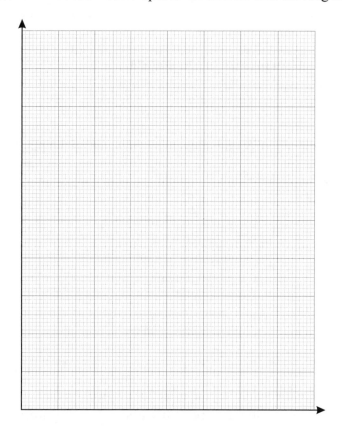

[2]

c) Describe the relationship between air flow around the plant and transpiration rate.

....

[1]

d) Explain the effect of air flow on the rate of transpiration.

....

....

....

[2]

e) Assuming that the mean rate of water uptake is equal to the mean rate of transpiration, calculate the rate of transpiration for the plant in moving air. Give your answer in cm^3 hour^{-1}.

.... cm^3 hour^{-1}

[2]

[Total 8 marks]

Topic 6 — Plant Structures and Their Functions

Adaptations of Leaves and Plants

1 A student took leaves from three different species of plant and used a microscope to estimate the number of stomata on each leaf. The mean number of stomata per mm² for each species is shown in **Figure 2**.

Figure 2

Plant	A	B	C
Mean number of stomata mm^{-2}	463	212	55

a) Which plant (**A-C**) is most likely to be adapted to living in a dry environment? Explain your answer.

....

....

....

[3]

b) Apart from number of stomata, give **one** other adaptation a plant may have to living in a dry environment.

....

[1]

[Total 4 marks]

2* Leaves are specialised structures adapted to capture light and carry out photosynthesis for the rest of the plant.

Explain how a leaf is adapted to maximise photosynthesis.

....

....

....

....

....

....

....

....

....

....

....

[Total 6 marks]

Plant Hormones

For each of the following sentences, state whether they are true or false.

Positive gravitropism is growth away from gravity. ....

Negative gravitropism is growth away from gravity. ....

Negative phototropism is growth towards a light source. ....

Positive phototropism is growth towards a light source. ....

1   Two sets of cress seedlings were allowed to germinate under identical environmental conditions. **Grade 6-7**

When the newly germinated shoots were 3 cm tall, the two sets of seedlings were treated as follows:

*   The cress seedlings in **Set A** received light from all sides.
*   The cress seedlings in **Set B** were placed in a box with a slit in one side, so that they received light from one side only.

The results are shown in **Figure 1**.

Figure 1

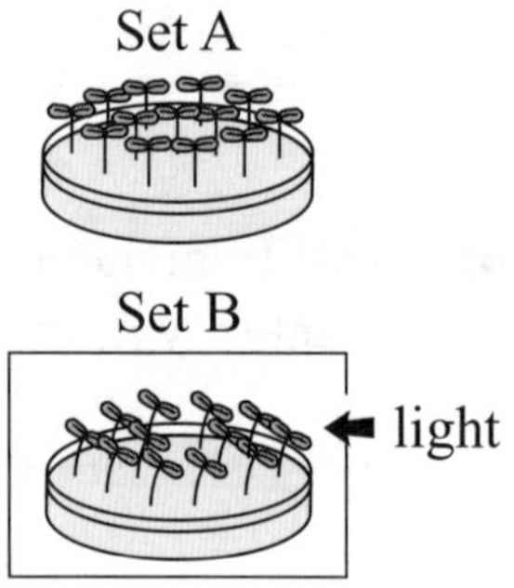

Set A

Set B

← light

a) Compare the growth of the seedlings in Set A with those in Set B.

....

....

[1]

b) Suggest **one** advantage to the plant of this response.

....

[1]

Auxin is a hormone that controls the growth of a plant in response to light.

c) Explain the results for **Set B**. Refer to the influence of auxin in your answer.

....

....

....

[2]

d) Explain how the action of auxin is different in the roots and shoots of a plant.

....

....

[2]

[Total 6 marks]

Commercial Uses of Plant Hormones

1 The ripeness of a fruit can affect how likely a customer is to buy it. *(Grade 4-6)*

a) Which of the following chemicals (**A-D**) causes fruit to ripen?

☐ **A** ethene ☐ **C** ethanol

☐ **B** gibberellin ☐ **D** insulin

[1]

b) The bananas we buy in supermarkets usually come from countries abroad, such as Ecuador and Colombia. Explain why bananas sold in UK supermarkets are often picked before they are ripe.

....

....

[2]

[Total 3 marks]

2 Many different plant growth hormones are involved in the growth and development of a plant. **Figure 1** shows the early stages of development of a seed. *(Grade 6-7)*

Figure 1

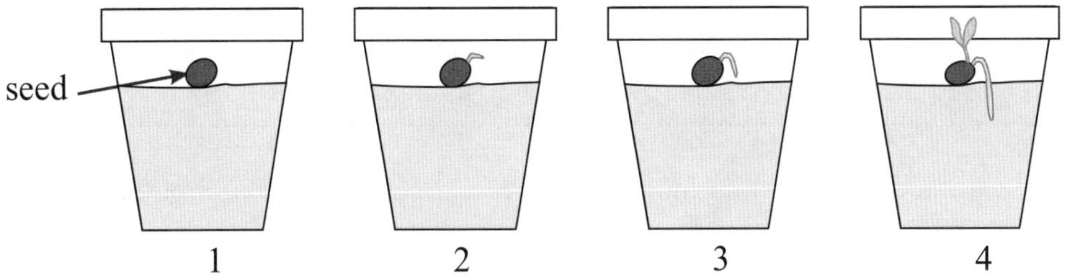

a) i) What is the name of the developmental process shown in **Figure 1**?

....

[1]

ii) Name **one** plant hormone which can be used commercially to start this process in some seeds.

....

[1]

b) i) Which additional hormone is likely to be involved in **stage 4** of **Figure 1**? Explain your answer.

....

....

[2]

ii) Give **one** commercial use of this hormone.

....

[1]

[Total 5 marks]

Topic 6 — Plant Structures and Their Functions

3 Farmers often spray their narrow-leaved crops with a selective weedkiller. This kills the weeds growing around the crops, but not the crops themselves.

Grade 6-7

a) Name **one** plant hormone that would be present in the selective weedkiller.

....

[1]

b) Explain why this hormone can kill the weeds but does not affect the crops.

....

....

[2]

[Total 3 marks]

Figure 2

4* **Figure 2** shows grapes growing on a vine. In many countries, manufactured gibberellins are used to help grow large, seedless varieties of fruit, which can be grown all year round.

Grade 7-9

Suggest and explain how gibberellins might be used to help grow large, high quality, seedless grapes, which can be grown all year round.

....

....

....

....

....

....

....

....

....

....

....

[Total 6 marks]

Exam Practice Tip

Make a list of all the plant hormones you know and the roles of each of them. Remember, some plant hormones have more than one role and sometimes these roles overlap, e.g auxins and gibberellins both have roles in plant growth.

Topic 6 — Plant Structures and Their Functions

Hormones

1 The endocrine system is a collection of glands in the body that secrete hormones. **Grade 4-6**

a) Endocrine glands secrete hormones directly into

☐ **A** cells ☐ **B** tissues ☐ **C** blood ☐ **D** organs

[1]

b) Hormones are

☐ **A** tissues ☐ **B** cells ☐ **C** chemicals ☐ **D** enzymes

[1]

c) **Figure 1** shows the positions of some glands in the human body. Name glands A to E in **Figure 1**.

Figure 1

A ....

B ....

C ....

D ....

E ....

[5]

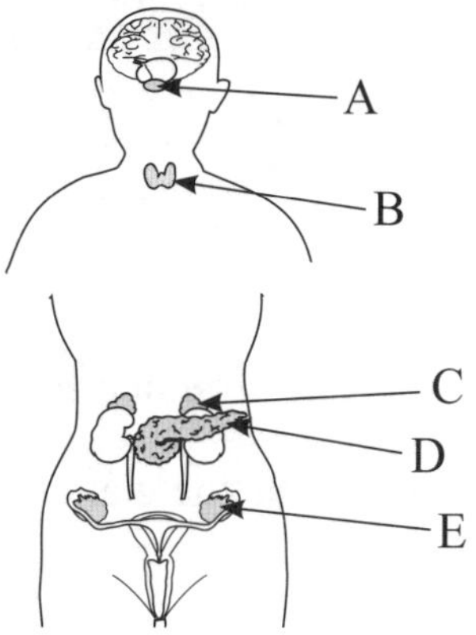

d) State **two** ways in which communication via the endocrine system differs from communication via the nervous system.

1. ....

2. ....

[2]

[Total 9 marks]

2 Males produce a greater amount of testosterone than females. One of the consequences of this, is that males' bones are more dense than females' bones. **Grade 6-7**

a) Based on the information above, name **one** of testosterone's target organs.

....

[1]

b) A possible treatment for prostate cancer is to have the testes removed. Explain why men who have had their testes removed are more at risk of developing brittle bones.

....

....

....

[2]

[Total 3 marks]

Adrenaline and Thyroxine

The graph below shows the change in the level of a hormone controlled by a negative feedback response over time.
Use the words on the right to fill in the labels on the graph.

normal   increase in   stimulated

inhibited   decrease in

.... level of hormone detected

Blood hormone level

release of hormone ....

.... level of hormone

Time

.... level of hormone detected

release of hormone ....

1 The hormone adrenaline is produced in times of fear or stress. `Grade 4-6`

a) Name the glands that release adrenaline.

....

[1]

b) Give **one** effect that adrenaline has on the body.

....

[1]

c) Name the response that adrenaline prepares the body for.

....

[1]

[Total 3 marks]

2 Thyroxine is a hormone. `Grade 6-7`

a) State **one** role of thyroxine in the body.

....

[1]

b) Explain how the body prevents the level of thyroxine in the blood from getting too high.

....

....

....

....

[3]

[Total 4 marks]

Topic 7 — Animal Coordination, Control and Homeostasis

The Menstrual Cycle

1 Oestrogen is a hormone involved in the menstrual cycle. (Grade 4-6)

a) Name the gland that releases oestrogen.

....

[1]

b) Name the hormone that stimulates oestrogen production.

....

[1]

c) Describe how oestrogen effects the uterus lining.

....

[1]

[Total 3 marks]

2 **Figure 1** shows how levels of four different hormones change during the menstrual cycle. (Grade 6-7)

Figure 1

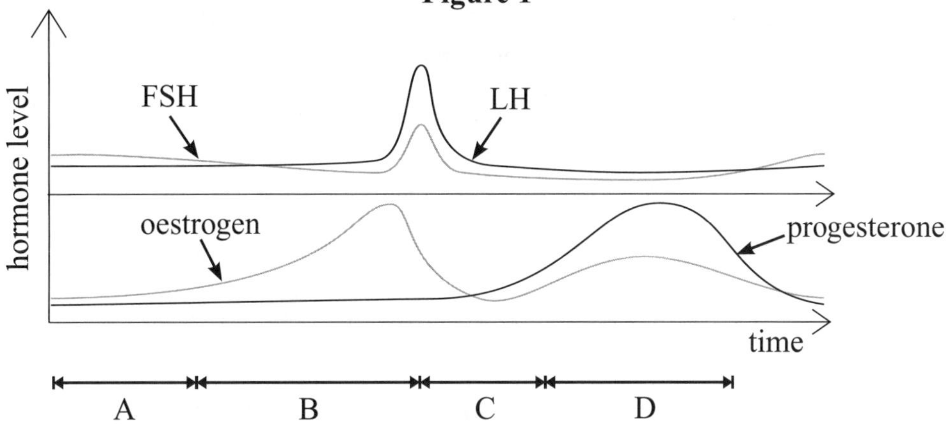

a) During which time period marked on **Figure 1** does menstruation occur?

☐ **A**   ☐ **B**   ☐ **C**   ☐ **D**

[1]

b) Add an arrow (↑) to the *x*-axis on **Figure 1**, to show the time at which ovulation occurs.

[1]

c) Before ovulation can occur, a follicle must mature. Name the hormone that causes this.

....

[1]

d) Explain how the uterus lining is maintained in the days after ovulation.

....

....

....

[3]

[Total 6 marks]

 ☐   ☐   ☐   Topic 7 — Animal Coordination, Control and Homeostasis

Controlling Fertility

1   Many people choose barrier methods of contraception to prevent pregnancy.   (Grade 4-6)

   a)   Give **one** example of a barrier method of contraception.

....

[1]

   b)   Describe how barrier methods of contraception work.

....

[1]

   c)   Give **two** advantages of barrier methods of contraception over hormonal methods of contraception.

    1. ....

    2. ....

[2]

[Total 4 marks]

2   Polycystic ovarian syndrome (PCOS) is a common cause of infertility in women. Women with the disorder don't ovulate regularly.   (Grade 6-7)

   a)   Explain why a woman with PCOS may find it hard to get pregnant.

....

....

....

[1]

   b)   Explain how clomifene therapy could help a woman with PCOS become pregnant.

....

....

....

[3]

   c)   If clomifene therapy doesn't help the woman to become pregnant, multiple eggs could be collected from the woman's ovaries and then fertilised using the man's sperm. One or two of the resulting embryos could then be transferred to the woman's uterus.

    i)   State the name given to this process.

....

[1]

    ii)   Explain why hormones are given to the woman at the beginning of this process.

....

[1]

[Total 6 marks]

Topic 7 — Animal Coordination, Control and Homeostasis

3 Some methods of hormonal contraception use oestrogen to help prevent pregnancy.

Grade 6-7

a) Explain how oestrogen in hormonal contraceptives helps to prevent pregnancy.

....

....

[2]

b) Many people prefer to use hormonal methods of contraception rather than barrier methods.
Give **two** advantages of hormonal methods of contraception over barrier methods of contraception.

1. ....

2. ....

[2]

[Total 4 marks]

4 The mini pill is a method of oral contraception. It contains progesterone and needs to be taken around the same time every day.

Grade 6-7

a) Many women who take the mini pill don't ovulate.

i) Explain how taking the mini pill may prevent ovulation.

....

....

....

[3]

ii) It's not only the effect on ovulation that makes the mini pill an effective contraceptive.
Explain **one** other way in which the mini pill can prevent pregnancy.

....

....

[2]

b) Although the mini pill is an effective method of contraceptive, a couple may still be advised to use a condom during intercourse. Suggest why.

....

[1]

c) The contraceptive implant is a small tube, which is inserted beneath the skin of the arm and continuously releases progesterone. It is effective for three years. Suggest **one** reason why a woman may choose to have a contraceptive implant rather than using the mini pill.

....

[1]

[Total 7 marks]

Exam Practice Tip

Knowing the roles of the hormones that control the menstrual cycle is really important when it comes to understanding how these hormones are used to control fertility. So make sure you've got it all sorted out in your head.

     Topic 7 — Animal Coordination, Control and Homeostasis

Homeostasis — Control of Blood Glucose

1 Homeostasis involves the regulation of blood glucose concentration. **Grade 4-6**

a) Explain what is meant by the term 'homeostasis'.

....
[1]

b) Name the gland in the body that monitors and controls blood glucose concentration.

....
[1]

[Total 2 marks]

2 In an experiment, the blood glucose concentration of a person was recorded at regular intervals in a 90 minute time period. Fifteen minutes into the experiment, a glucose drink was given. **Figure 1** shows the results of the experiment. **Grade 7-9**

Figure 1

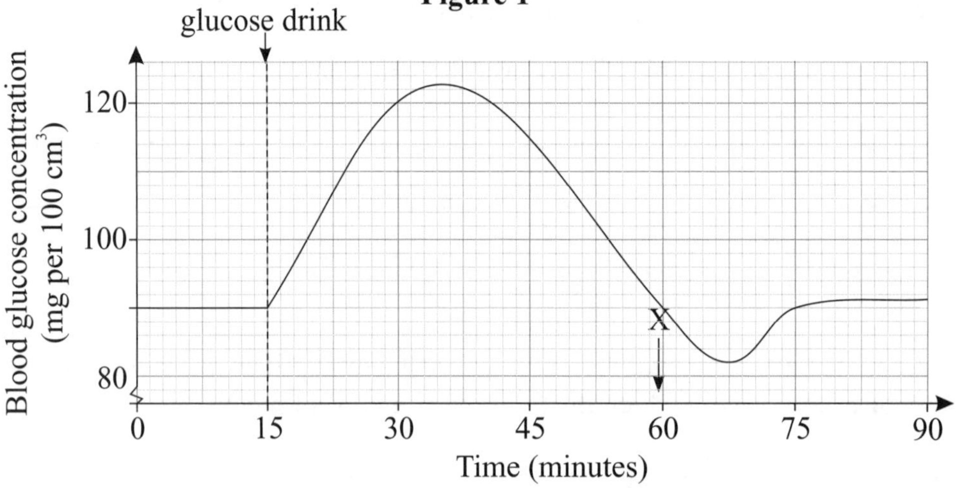

Graph: y-axis labelled "Blood glucose concentration (mg per 100 cm³)" ranging from 80 to 120; x-axis labelled "Time (minutes)" from 0 to 90. A "glucose drink" arrow points to 15 minutes. The curve stays flat at ~90 until 15 min, rises to a peak of ~123 around 35 min, falls to a minimum at point X (~60-70 min) and returns to ~90.

a) Explain what is happening to the blood glucose concentration between 15 and 60 minutes.

....

....

....
[3]

b) i) Name the hormone being released by the pancreas at point **X** on the graph.

....
[1]

ii) Explain how the hormone released at point **X** affects the blood glucose concentration.

....

....

....
[3]

[Total 7 marks]

Topic 7 — Animal Coordination, Control and Homeostasis

Diabetes

1 A patient visits her health centre because she is concerned she is at risk of developing type 2 diabetes.

Grade 6-7

a) i) Firstly, a nurse measures the patient's mass and height. Explain why he does this.

....

....

[2]

ii) Next the nurse uses his tape measure to take **two** other measurements of the patient's body. Suggest which two measurements he takes. Explain your answer.

....

....

....

[3]

b) Give **two** treatments that the patient's doctor might recommend if the patient was later diagnosed with type 2 diabetes.

1. ....

2. ....

[2]

c) Describe the underlying causes of type 2 diabetes.

....

....

[2]

[Total 9 marks]

2 In rare cases, type 1 diabetes may be treated with a pancreas transplant.

Grade 7-9

a) i) Explain why a pancreas transplant could be used to treat a person with type 1 diabetes.

....

....

[2]

ii) Suggest **one** reason why a pancreas transplant is rarely used to treat type 1 diabetes.

....

....

[1]

b) State the main form of treatment for type 1 diabetes.

....

[1]

[Total 5 marks]

    Topic 7 — Animal Coordination, Control and Homeostasis

Thermoregulation

1   The thermoregulatory centre in the hypothalamus monitors and controls body temperature.   Grade 4-6

   a) It's important that core body temperature remains around 37 °C so that:

   ☐ **A** hormones can circulate freely.   ☐ **C** blood glucose concentration remains constant.

   ☐ **B** pathogens can't enter the body.   ☐ **D** enzymes can work effectively.

   [1]

   b) What are the receptors in the thermoregulatory centre used to monitor?

   ....

   [1]

   c) Briefly describe how the thermoregulatory centre receives information about external temperature.

   ....

   ....

   [2]

   [Total 4 marks]

2   Sweating, vasodilation and shivering are all mechanisms used in thermoregulation.   Grade 6-7

   a) i) Describe the role of the dermis and epidermis during sweating.

   Dermis: ....

   Epidermis: ....

   [2]

   ii) Explain how sweating helps to cool the body down.

   ....

   ....

   [2]

   b) Explain how the mechanisms of vasoconstriction and shivering are used in thermoregulation.

   Vasoconstriction: ....

   ....

   ....

   Shivering: ....

   ....

   ....

   [6]

   [Total 10 marks]

Exam Practice Tip

In the exam, you might be asked to explain how the body's thermoregulatory system would respond in a certain situation, e.g. during a cycle race. For these questions, think about what's happening to the body's temperature — if it's going up (e.g. because increased respiration is warming the body), it's going to need to be brought back down, and vice versa.

Topic 7 — Animal Coordination, Control and Homeostasis

Osmoregulation and The Kidneys

Circle the correct underlined word in each sentence below to make the passage correct.

Osmoregulation is regulation of the amount of <u>blood/water</u> in the body.

The wrong amount of water in the blood can damage <u>cells/enzymes</u> because

it causes them to lose or gain too much water by <u>osmosis/diffusion</u>.

The amount of water and ions in the body is controlled by the <u>pancreas/kidneys</u>.

---

1   **Figure 1** shows the structure of a nephron.   Grade 4-6

Figure 1

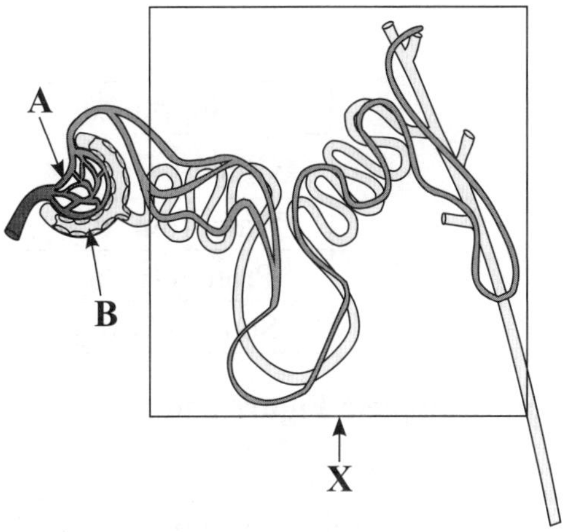

a) Name the parts labelled **A** and **B** on **Figure 1**.

A: ....

B: ....

[2]

b) Describe what happens to ions and water in the section
of the nephron labelled **X** on **Figure 1**.

....

....

[1]

c) Glucose moves from the liquid in a nephron into the blood by the process of

☐ **A** diffusion   ☐ **C** selective reabsorption

☐ **B** osmosis   ☐ **D** ultrafiltration

[1]

d) Urea is removed from the blood by the kidneys. Briefly describe how urea is created by the body.

....

....

[1]

e) Describe the passage of urine from the nephrons in the kidneys to where it is expelled by the body.

....

....

....

....

[4]

[Total 9 marks]

2 Osmoregulation is important to keep cells functioning normally. Explain how the structure of body cells could be affected if osmoregulation mechanisms failed to work properly.

Grade 6-7

....

....

....

....

....

[Total 4 marks]

3 The kidneys are important for controlling the concentration of different substances in the blood.

Grade 7-9

Figure 2 shows the amount of four different substances that are filtered by the kidneys in a healthy adult each day. It also show the percentage of each substance that is reabsorbed into the blood.

Figure 2

Substance	Amount filtered	Amount reabsorbed (%)
Glucose (g day^{-1})	180	....
Water (dm^3 day^{-1})	180	99.2
Protein (g day^{-1})	0	n/a
Sodium (g day^{-1})	575	99.5

a) Complete **Figure 2** to give the percentage of glucose reabsorbed.

[1]

b) Explain why the amount of protein filtered by the kidneys is 0 g day^{-1}.

....

[1]

c) Write the names of the four substances from **Figure 2** in the correct column in the table below.

Concentration of the substance is the **same** in the renal vein as it is in the renal artery.	Concentration of the substance is **lower** in the renal vein than it is in the renal artery.
....	....
....	....

[2]

d) Calculate how much water is lost in the urine each day.

.... dm^3 day^{-1}

[3]

[Total 7 marks]

Topic 7 — Animal Coordination, Control and Homeostasis

More on The Kidneys

Fill in the gaps in this passage using words on the right. Words may be used more than once or not at all.

pituitary   water   thyroid

less   more   sodium

When the brain detects a drop in the water content of the blood, the .... gland

releases .... ADH. This makes the collecting ducts .... permeable,

so the kidneys reabsorb more ....

1   A person with kidney failure can be treated with dialysis. This involves a person's blood flowing through a machine, alongside specialist dialysis fluid.   **Grade 6-7**

a) Briefly describe what happens inside the dialysis machine.

....

....

[2]

b) Explain why it is important that the dialysis fluid has the same concentration of dissolved substances as healthy blood.

....

[1]

c) Dialysis will not cure kidney failure.

i) State a procedure that can cure kidney failure. ....

[1]

ii) Suggest **one** reason why a person may remain on dialysis for many years rather than undergoing the procedure that would cure them.

....

....

[1]

[Total 5 marks]

2   Cranial diabetes insipidus is a disorder in which the body does not produce enough anti-diuretic hormone (ADH). Explain how having cranial diabetes insipidus may affect the amount of water a person needs to drink each day.   **Grade 7-9**

....

....

....

....

....

[Total 4 marks]

     Topic 7 — Animal Coordination, Control and Homeostasis

Exchange of Materials

1 Sticklebacks are a type of freshwater fish. They have specialised exchange surfaces, called gills, and a mass transport system powered by a heart.

Grade 6-7

a) Give **two** substances that a stickleback must transport into its body in order to survive.

....

[2]

b) Explain why a stickleback needs both specialised exchange surfaces and a mass transport system in order to survive.

....

....

....

....

....

....

[4]

[Total 6 marks]

2 A student was investigating the effect of size on the uptake of substances by diffusion. He cut different sized cubes of agar containing universal indicator and placed them in beakers of acid. He timed how long it took for the acid to diffuse through to the centre of each cube (and so change the colour of the agar).

Grade 7-9

Figure 1 shows the relationship between the surface area and volume of the agar cubes.

Figure 1

Cube size (cm)	Surface area (cm²)	Volume (cm³)	Simple ratio
2 × 2 × 2	24	8	3:1
3 × 3 × 3	**X**	**Y**	2:1
5 × 5 × 5	150	125	**Z** : 1

a) Calculate the values of X, Y and Z in **Figure 1**.

X = ... cm²

Y = ... cm³

Z = ...

[3]

b) Explain which cube would take the longest to change colour.

....

....

[1]

[Total 4 marks]

Diffusion and the Alveoli

1 Fick's Law describes the relationship between the rate of diffusion and the factors that affect it.

a) Complete the following to state Fick's Law for the rate of diffusion across a membrane:

$$\text{Rate of diffusion } \alpha \ \frac{\text{surface area} \times \text{...}}{\text{...}}$$

[2]

b) A scientist is investigating the effects of different factors on the rate of diffusion of carbon dioxide across a cell membrane. Using Fick's Law, state how the rate of diffusion of carbon dioxide would change if the surface area of the cell was doubled and all other factors were kept the same.

....

[1]

[Total 3 marks]

2 A scientist investigated the diffusion of ammonia along a glass tube. **Figure 1** shows the apparatus she used.

Figure 1

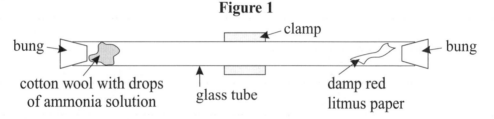

When the ammonia reaches the end of the tube, the litmus paper changes colour. The scientist timed how long this colour change took at five different concentrations of ammonia. **Figure 2** shows her results.

Figure 2

Concentration of ammonia (number of drops)	1	2	3	4	5
Time (s)	46	35	28	19	12

a) State what the results in **Figure 2** show about the effect of concentration on the rate of diffusion.

....

[1]

b) State **two** factors, other than concentration gradient, that affect the rate of diffusion into a cell.

1. ....

2. ....

[2]

c) Suggest **one** way in which the scientist could increase the precision of her results.

....

[1]

[Total 4 marks]

Topic 8 — Exchange and Transport in Animals

3   **Figure 3** shows an alveolus in the lungs.   (Grade 6-7)

Figure 3

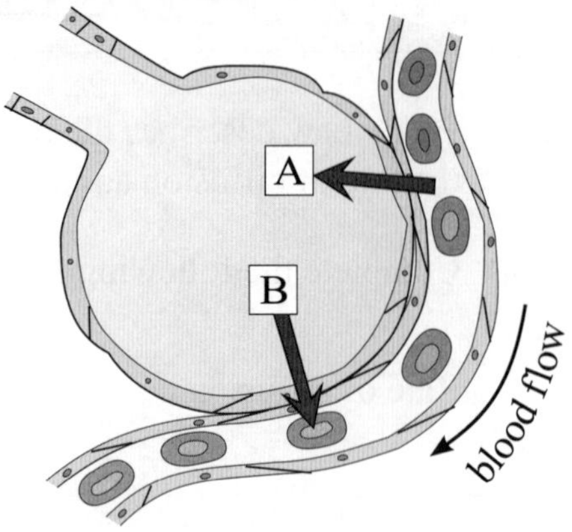

a) Name the gases A and B.

A ....

B ....

[2]

b) Gases A and B move down their concentration gradients by diffusion. Explain how the blood flow at an alveolus ensures there is a high rate of diffusion for both gases following the inhalation of air.

....

....

....

....

....

[3]

c) Other than a good blood supply, explain **two** ways in which alveoli in the lungs are adapted for gas exchange.

1. ....

....

2. ....

....

[4]

[Total 9 marks]

4   Emphysema is a disease which results in fewer alveoli in the lungs.   (Grade 7-9)

Explain why a person with emphysema may have to breathe more rapidly to deliver enough oxygen to their body cells.

....

....

....

....

....

....

[Total 3 marks]

Circulatory System — Blood

1 The blood is composed of different components, each of which has a different function. Grade 4-6

a) Which of the following are types of white blood cell?

☐ **A** phagoctytes and lysozymes   ☐ **C** phagoctytes and erythrocytes

☐ **B** phagoctytes and lymphocytes   ☐ **D** erythrocytes and lymphocytes

[1]

b) Name the component of the blood that produces antibodies.

....

[1]

c) Describe the structure and function of blood plasma.

....

....

[2]

[Total 4 marks]

2 The components of blood can be separated by spinning them at high speed. **Figure 1** shows a tube of blood that has been separated in this way. Grade 6-7

Figure 1

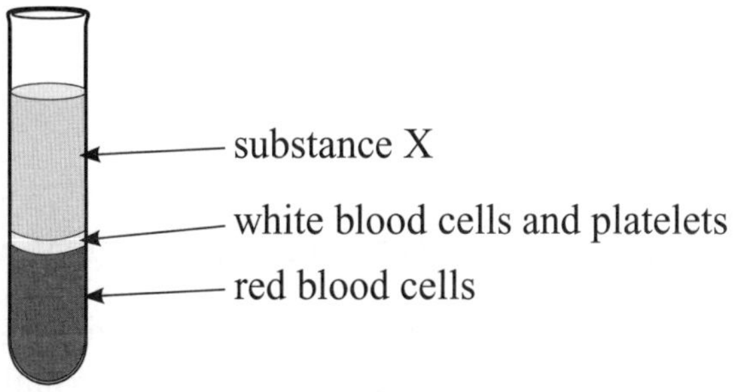

— substance X

— white blood cells and platelets

— red blood cells

a) Identify the substance labelled X in **Figure 1**.

....

[1]

b) Red blood cells have a biconcave shape. Explain how this allows them to fulfil their function.

....

....

[2]

c) A scientist analysing the blood sample found that it had a lower than normal concentration of platelets. Explain one problem the patient may experience due to this.

....

....

....

[2]

[Total 5 marks]

Topic 8 — Exchange and Transport in Animals

Circulatory System — Blood Vessels

Label each of the following diagrams to indicate whether they represent a capillary, artery or vein.

Diagrams
not to
scale.

A. ....   B. ....   C. ....

1   Blood vessels can be identified by their structure or location in the body.   (Grade 4-6)

   a) i) Name the type of blood vessel that has valves.

      ....
      [1]

      ii) Describe the purpose of valves in a blood vessel.

      ....
      [1]

   b) Name the type of blood vessel that joins up to form veins.

      ....
      [1]

      [Total 3 marks]

2   Different types of blood vessel perform different functions.   (Grade 6-7)

   a) Veins and arteries both have a layer of smooth muscle within their walls. Which of these types of
      blood vessel has a thicker layer of muscle? Explain your answer with reference to their functions.

      ....
      ....
      ....
      ....
      [4]

   b) Capillaries are very narrow. Explain how this allows them to fulfil their function.

      ....
      ....
      [2]

      [Total 6 marks]

Exam Practice Tip

There are lots of places in this topic where you could be asked how the structure of something is related to its function.
In these sorts of questions, don't just describe the function then rattle off what it looks like — make sure you clearly
explain how each structural feature you mention helps with the function.

Topic 8 — Exchange and Transport in Animals

Circulatory System — Heart

Complete the following passage by circling the correct bold word or phrase in each sentence.

Deoxygenated / oxygenated blood enters the right atrium through the **vena cava / aorta**.

From there it is pumped into the **right ventricle / pulmonary vein**. Then it is pumped

up through the pulmonary **vein / artery** towards the **lungs / rest of the body**.

A **valve / low pressure** prevents the blood from flowing back into the right atrium.

1 The heart pumps blood around the body. **Figure 1** shows a diagram of the heart.

Figure 1

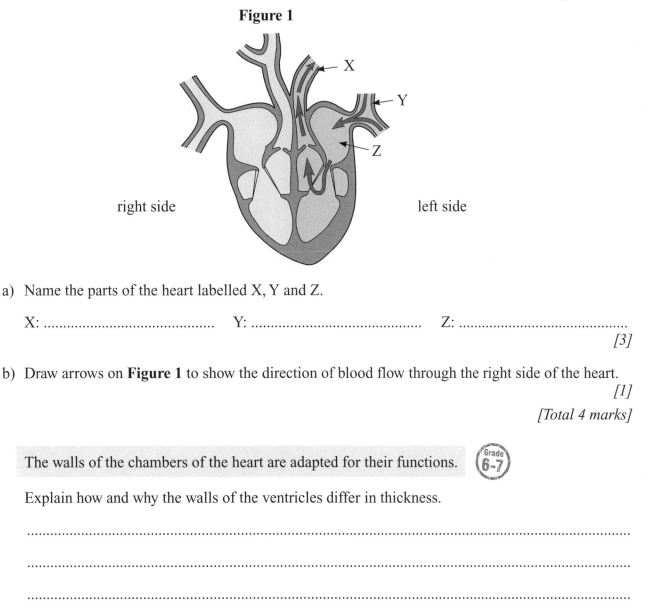

right side   left side

a) Name the parts of the heart labelled X, Y and Z.

X: .... Y: .... Z: ....

[3]

b) Draw arrows on **Figure 1** to show the direction of blood flow through the right side of the heart.

[1]

[Total 4 marks]

2 The walls of the chambers of the heart are adapted for their functions.

Explain how and why the walls of the ventricles differ in thickness.

....

....

....

....

....

[Total 3 marks]

Topic 8 — Exchange and Transport in Animals

3   A scientist was investigating the effect of height on cardiac output in athletes. He predicted that taller athletes would have a greater cardiac output than shorter athletes, as taller athletes are likely to have larger hearts. Before he measured their heights, the scientist measured the stroke volume and resting heart rate of each athlete, and calculated their cardiac output. His results for two of the athletes are shown in **Figure 2**.

Figure 2

Athlete	1	2
Heart rate (bpm)	57	**Y**
Stroke volume (cm³)	84	65
Cardiac output (cm³ min⁻¹)	**X**	4095

a) Explain what is meant by the term 'stroke volume'.

....

....

[1]

b) Calculate the cardiac output for Athlete **1**.

Cardiac output = ... cm³ min⁻¹

[2]

c) Calculate the heart rate for Athlete **2**.

Heart rate = ... bpm

[2]

d) Suggest an explanation as to why the scientist predicted that a larger heart would result in a greater cardiac output.

....

....

....

....

....

[3]

e) The scientist asks the athletes to cycle for 10 minutes to increase their heart rate. Explain how exercise will affect the athletes' cardiac output.

....

[1]

[Total 9 marks]

Exam Practice Tip

The structure of the heart and the way blood flows through it can be pretty tricky to get your head around. In the exam you might find it helpful to sketch a quick diagram of the heart and the way blood flows through it to help you answer questions on it. Make sure you really know how to calculate heart rate, stroke volume and cardiac output too.

Respiration

1 Respiration is an exothermic reaction. It can occur either aerobically or anaerobically. **Grade 6-7**

a) What does it mean if a reaction is exothermic?

☐ **A** It releases energy to the environment.

☐ **B** It produces carbon dioxide.

☐ **C** It takes in energy from the environment.

☐ **D** It is used in metabolism.

[1]

b) Explain why respiration reactions are essential for the life of an organism.

....

....

[2]

c) i) Name a substance that is broken down in both aerobic and anaerobic respiration.

....

[1]

ii) Name a substance that is broken down in aerobic respiration but not in anaerobic respiration.

....

[1]

iii) Name the products of aerobic respiration.

....

[2]

d) Give **one** reason why it may be more beneficial for the body to use aerobic respiration to transfer energy most of the time, rather than using anaerobic respiration.

....

....

[1]

e) Give **one** example of a situation in which a person may begin to respire anaerobically.

....

[1]

f) Describe how the products of anaerobic respiration differ between plants and animals.

....

....

....

[3]

[Total 12 marks]

Topic 8 — Exchange and Transport in Animals

2   The air that a person inhales has a different composition from the air that they exhale.
    Figure 1 shows the percentages of different gases in the inhaled air and in the exhaled air.

a) Explain the difference in the values for the
    percentage of oxygen in inhaled and exhaled air.

Figure 1

	Inhaled air (%)	Exhaled air (%)
Nitrogen	78	78
Oxygen	21	16
Carbon dioxide		
Other gases	0.9	0.9

....

....

....

....

[1]

b) Explain how the percentage of carbon dioxide would differ between inhaled and exhaled air.

....

....

[2]

[Total 3 marks]

3   A scientist was measuring the effects of exercise on respiration. He asked a male
    volunteer to jog for 10 minutes on a treadmill. The speed of the treadmill was increased
    over the course of the 10 minutes, so that he was gradually working harder, until at the
    end he felt unable to do any more exercise. **Figure 2** shows the oxygen consumption
    (the amount of oxygen used by the body per minute) of the man during the exercise.

Figure 2

oxygen consumption (ml kg^{-1} min^{-1}) vs time (minutes)

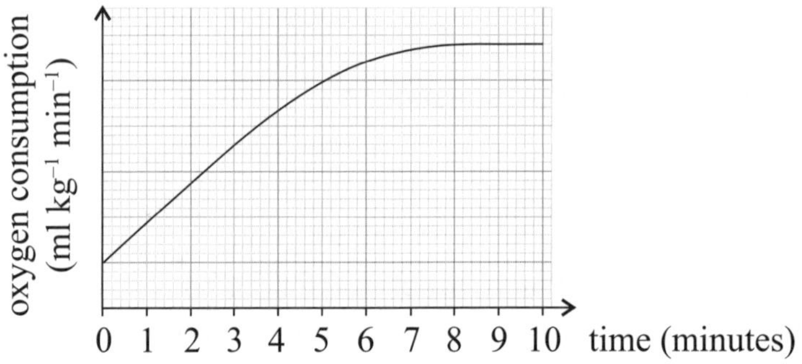

a) Describe how oxygen consumption changed during the exercise.

....

....

[2]

b) In the final two minutes of the exercise, the man was respiring anaerobically.
    Explain how the scientist may know this by looking at the graph in **Figure 2**.

....

....

....

....

[2]

[Total 4 marks]

Topic 8 — Exchange and Transport in Animals

Investigating Respiration

1 An experiment was set up using two sealed beakers, each with a carbon dioxide monitor attached. The set up is shown in **Figure 1**.

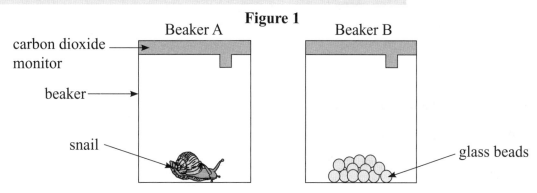

Figure 1

The percentage (%) of carbon dioxide in the air in both beakers was measured at the start of the experiment and again after 2 hours. The results are shown in **Figure 2**.

Figure 2

Time	% carbon dioxide in the air	
(hours)	Beaker A	Beaker B
0	0.04	0.04
2	0.10	0.04

a) Suggest **one** ethical consideration that must be taken into account during this experiment.

....

[1]

b) Explain the purpose of the glass beads in Beaker B.

....

....

[2]

c) Explain the results for Beaker A.

....

....

[1]

d) Explain how the level of oxygen in Beaker A would have changed during the experiment.

....

....

[2]

e) Suggest how the internal temperature of Beaker A would differ from that of Beaker B during the experiment. Explain your answer.

....

....

....

[2]

[Total 8 marks]

Topic 8 — Exchange and Transport in Animals

Ecosystems & Interactions Between Organisms

Warm-Up

Put the words below into the correct column in the table, according to whether they are abiotic or biotic factors in an organism's environment.

Abiotic	Biotic

pollutants   light intensity   water

temperature   prey species

competition   predators

---

1 There are different levels of organisation within a habitat. *(Grade 4-6)*

a) A community is

☐ **A** all the organisms of one species living in a habitat.

☐ **B** all the organisms of different species living in a habitat.

☐ **C** all the organisms of one population living in a habitat.

☐ **D** all of the abiotic and biotic factors in an habitat.

[1]

b) Explain what is meant by the term 'ecosystem'.

....

[1]

[Total 2 marks]

---

2 Grasses make their own food by photosynthesis. In grassland communities, the grass leaves provide insects with shelter, a place to breed and a source of food. Visiting birds feed on insects. *(Grade 6-7)*

a) Explain what you would expect to happen to the birds visiting the grassland if a new insect predator entered the ecosystem.

....

....

[2]

b) The number of birds visiting the grassland decreases. What would you eventually expect to happen to the number of grass plants? Explain your answer.

....

....

....

[3]

[Total 5 marks]

3 A cuckoo is a type of bird that lays its eggs in the nest of another bird. When the cuckoo egg hatches, the cuckoo chick kills some of the offspring of the host and the host bird raises the cuckoo chick as if it was its own.

Grade 6-7

a) Name the type of interaction between a cuckoo chick and its host. Explain your answer.

....

....

[2]

b) Ants often live in the hollow thorns on a certain species of tree. The ants living in the trees feed on the trees' nectar. When herbivores try to graze on the trees, the ants bite them. Some ant species have also been shown to protect the trees from harmful bacteria.

Which of the following statements best describes the relationship between the ants and the trees?

☐ **A** The ants are parasites because they depend entirely on the trees to survive.

☐ **B** The relationship is mutualistic because both the ants and the trees benefit from it.

☐ **C** The relationship is parasitic because the host is harmed and doesn't benefit from it.

☐ **D** The relationship is mutualistic because the trees depend on the ants to survive.

[1]

[Total 3 marks]

4 Prickly acacia is a tree species native to Africa, and parts of Asia. It was introduced to Australia many years ago. It has invaded large areas of land in the warmer parts of the country. The trees grow best in areas with a high average temperature and where there is plenty of water, such as along rivers or on flood plains where there is seasonal flooding.

Grade 6-7

a) Australia experienced particularly high rainfall in the 1950s and 1970s. Explain how the prickly acacia population in Australia may have changed during these periods.

....

....

[2]

b) Global temperature is thought to be increasing. What may happen to the distribution of prickly acacia in Australia over the next few decades? Explain your answer.

....

....

....

[2]

c) When prickly acacia invade an area it can negatively impact the populations of various grasses in that area. Explain why this might be the case.

....

....

[2]

[Total 6 marks]

Topic 9 — Ecosystems and Material Cycles

Investigating Ecosystems

1   A group of students used a 0.5 m² quadrat to investigate the number of buttercups growing in a field. They counted the number of buttercups in the quadrat in ten randomly selected places. **Figure 1** shows their results.

Figure 1

Quadrat Number	Number of buttercups
1	15
2	13
3	16
4	23
5	26
6	23
7	13
8	12
9	16
10	13

a)   i)   Explain why it is important that the quadrats were randomly placed in the field.

....
[1]

ii) Describe a method that could have been used to randomly place the quadrats.

....
[1]

b)   What is the modal number of buttercups in a quadrat in **Figure 1**?

.... buttercups
[1]

c)   What is the median number of buttercups in **Figure 1**?

.... buttercups
[1]

d)   Calculate the mean number of buttercups per 0.5 m² quadrat.

.... buttercups per 0.5 m²
[1]

e)   The total area of the field was 1750 m².
Estimate the number of buttercups in the whole of the field.

.... buttercups
[2]

[Total 7 marks]

2   A belt transect was carried out from the edge of a small pond, across a grassy field and into a woodland. The distributions of four species of plant were recorded along the transect, along with the soil moisture and light levels. **Figure 2** shows the results.

Figure 2

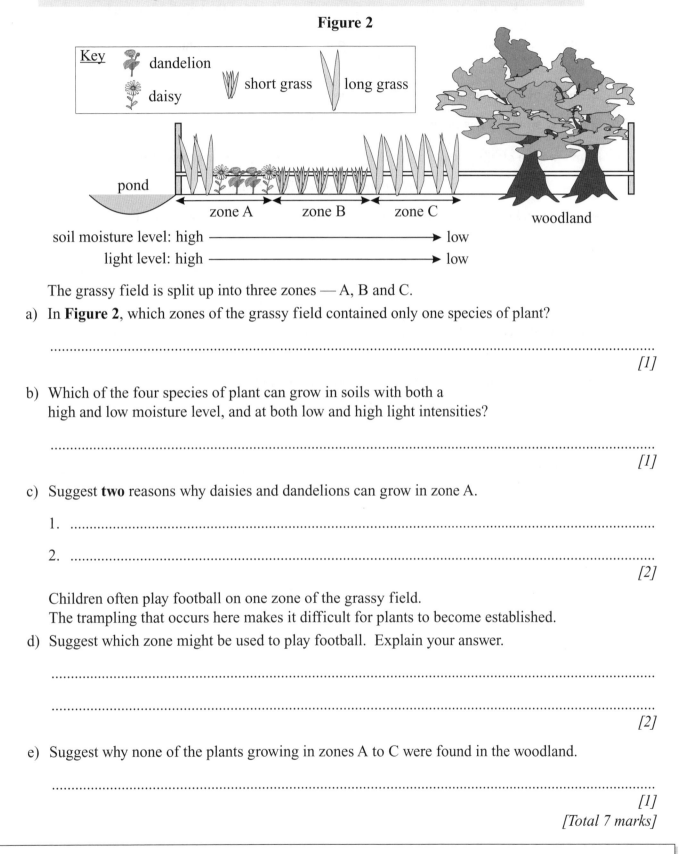

The grassy field is split up into three zones — A, B and C.

a) In **Figure 2**, which zones of the grassy field contained only one species of plant?

   ....

   [1]

b) Which of the four species of plant can grow in soils with both a high and low moisture level, and at both low and high light intensities?

   ....

   [1]

c) Suggest **two** reasons why daisies and dandelions can grow in zone A.

   1. ....

   2. ....

   [2]

   Children often play football on one zone of the grassy field.
   The trampling that occurs here makes it difficult for plants to become established.

d) Suggest which zone might be used to play football. Explain your answer.

   ....

   ....

   [2]

e) Suggest why none of the plants growing in zones A to C were found in the woodland.

   ....

   [1]
   [Total 7 marks]

Exam Practice Tip

Be careful with any calculations you're asked to make — the maths on the previous page isn't hard, but you need to make sure you don't mix up the mean, mode and median.

Topic 9 — Ecosystems and Material Cycles

Ecosystems and Energy Transfers

Warm-Up

Fill in the blanks in the text using words from below. Some of the words may not be needed.

lost   food   biomass   the Sun   gained   trophic level   animals

The mass of living material that makes up an organism is called ....

Energy is stored in this material.

Plants are the starting point for most food chains. They get their energy from

.... Energy passes along a food chain when ....

eat plants and each other. Energy is .... between each

.... in a food chain.

1   Pyramids of biomass can be constructed to represent the relative amount of biomass in each level of a food chain.

    Figure 1 shows a food chain from an area of oak woodland.
The biomass values are given in arbitrary units.

Figure 1

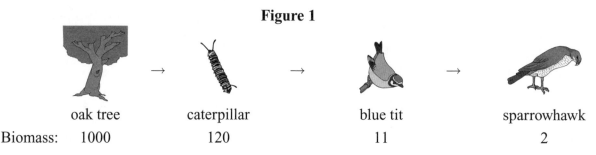

| | oak tree | caterpillar | blue tit | sparrowhawk |
| Biomass: | 1000 | 120 | 11 | 2 |

a) Use the biomass values given in **Figure 1** to construct a pyramid of biomass.

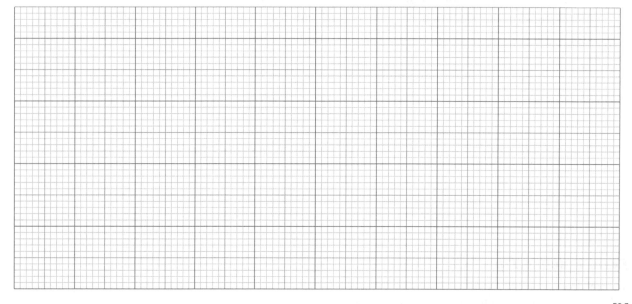

[2]

Topic 9 — Ecosystems and Material Cycles

b) Use the biomass values from **Figure 1** to suggest why there are usually only four or five trophic levels in a food chain.

....

....

[2]

[Total 4 marks]

2   There are energy losses at each trophic level in a food chain. **Figure 2** shows the amount of energy transferred between each trophic level in an ecosystem.   Grade **6-7**

Figure 2

Trophic Level	1	2	3	4
Energy transferred to next level (arbitrary units)	50 000	4000	360	36
Efficiency of energy transfer (%)	–	X	9	10

a) Calculate the value of **X** in **Figure 2**.

Efficiency of energy transfer = ... %

[2]

b) Calculate the mean efficiency of energy transfer between the trophic levels in **Figure 2**.

Mean efficiency of energy transfer = ... %

[1]

c) Explain why the efficiency of energy transfer between the trophic levels is so low.

....

....

....

....

....

[4]

[Total 7 marks]

Exam Practice Tip

You could be asked to draw something (like a pyramid of biomass) in the exam, so it's a good idea to always take a sharp pencil, ruler and eraser into the exam with you (as well as your lucky pen, of course). Other things that come in handy include: a calculator, a spare pen, a tissue, a bottle of water and a kitten (for the stress).

Topic 9 — Ecosystems and Material Cycles

Human Impacts on Biodiversity

1 Possums are a type of marsupial mammal native to Australia. In the 1800s they were introduced by humans into New Zealand for the fur trade.

Grade 6-7

Suggest **two** reasons why possums may have negatively affected species native to New Zealand.

1. ....

....

2. ....

....

[Total 2 marks]

2 Human interactions with ecosystems can change the abiotic conditions, reducing biodiversity.

a)* Explain how the application of fertilisers on farmland may reduce the biodiversity of nearby water sources.

Grade 7-9

....

....

....

....

....

....

....

....

[6]

b) Fish can be farmed in nets in the ocean. However, this method of fish farming can cause similar problems to excess fertilisers in surrounding waters. Suggest an explanation for this.

....

....

[2]

c) Explain **two** other potential impacts of open water fish farms on the biodiversity of their surrounding environment.

1. ....

....

2. ....

....

[2]

[Total 10 marks]

Topic 9 — Ecosystems and Material Cycles

Conservation and Biodiversity

1 Conservation efforts often aim to protect a single endangered species, e.g. the panda.

Grade 6-7

a) Explain **one** reason why efforts to protect one species may help to protect many others as well.

....

....

....

[2]

b) Suggest **one** reason why the protection of a species may benefit the economy of a country.

....

....

[1]

[Total 3 marks]

2* Human activity has reduced the forest cover in Ethiopia significantly. Land that used to be covered by trees is now more exposed to rainfall in the rainy season, leading to increased soil loss through erosion, and heat from the Sun during the dry season, leading to drought. Reforestation programmes employ local people to plant trees over large areas of land.

Grade 7-9

Discuss why reforestation may be beneficial for Ethiopia. Include details about the potential benefits for biodiversity, local farmers and Ethiopian society.

....

....

....

....

....

....

....

....

....

....

....

....

[Total 6 marks]

Food Security

1   Due to the increasing human population size, it is important to develop ways of producing food more sustainably.   *Grade 6-7*

a) Explain what is meant by the term 'sustainability'.

....

....

[1]

b) Give **one** reason why increasing fish consumption may not be sustainable.

....

....

[1]

c) Biofuels are more sustainable than fossil fuels, but can have a negative impact on food security. Explain how.

....

....

[1]

[Total 3 marks]

2   Human activities threaten global food security.   *Grade 6-7*

a) The Earth's temperature is increasing as a result of human activities. Explain why this could have a negative effect on food security in the future.

....

....

....

....

[3]

b) The use of pesticides on crops may lead to the evolution of new pests that are resistant to the pesticide. Explain why this might be a threat to food security.

....

....

[2]

c) Explain how an increase in the amount of animal farming is likely to impact food security.

....

....

....

....

[3]

[Total 8 marks]

Topic 9 — Ecosystems and Material Cycles

The Carbon Cycle

1   **Figure 1** shows an unfinished diagram of the carbon cycle.

Figure 1

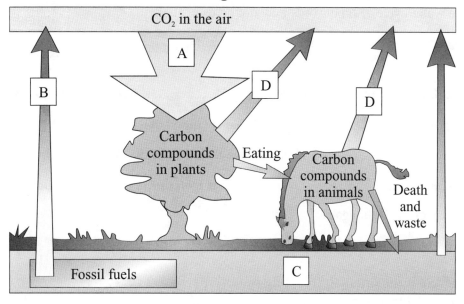

a) i) Name the process represented by **A** in **Figure 1**.

   ....

   [1]

   ii) Describe the importance of process **A** for an ecosystem.

   ....

   ....

   [1]

b) Name the process represented by **B** in **Figure 1**.

   ....

   [1]

c) Process **C** in **Figure 1** is decay. Describe the importance of decay in the carbon cycle.

   ....

   ....

   [2]

d) Give **one** biotic and **one** abiotic component of the ecosystem represented in **Figure 1**.

   Biotic: ....

   Abiotic: ....

   [2]

   [Total 7 marks]

Exam Practice Tip

In the exam you could be tested on any part of the carbon cycle, so make sure you know the whole of it and not just bits of it. Try sketching the whole cycle out and make sure you can link each bit together. Don't have your arrows going the wrong way round, and make sure you understand why the carbon is moving around, e.g. because of respiration. Sorted.

Topic 9 — Ecosystems and Material Cycles

The Water Cycle

Choose from the words below to complete the sentences about the water cycle. Some words may not be used at all.

precipitation   evaporate   warms   cools   water vapour   carbon dioxide   condense

Energy from the Sun makes water .... from the land and sea,

turning it into .... This is carried upwards. When it gets higher

up it .... and condenses to form clouds. Water falls from the

clouds as .... onto land. It then drains into the sea, before the

whole process starts again.

1   The water cycle is important in recycling water so that it is available for use by organisms.   Grade 4-6

a) Potable water is:

☐ **A** sea water.

☐ **B** drinking water.

☐ **C** contaminated water.

☐ **D** evaporated water.

[1]

b) Explain why sea water is not suitable for drinking by humans.

....

[1]

[Total 2 marks]

2   Somalia is a country on the eastern coast of Africa.
In 2011, a lack of rainfall in Somalia led to a severe drought.   Grade 7-9

Describe and explain **one** method of desalination which may
have been used in Somalia to provide water suitable for drinking.

....

....

....

....

....

....

[Total 4 marks]

Topic 9 — Ecosystems and Material Cycles

The Nitrogen Cycle

1   Nitrogen makes up roughly 78% of the gases in the atmosphere. Carbon dioxide makes up only 0.04%. Plants need to absorb both gases in order to survive and grow.

   a) Give **one** reason why plants need nitrogen in order to grow.

   ....

   [1]

   b) Plants absorb carbon dioxide from the air. Which of the following sentences (**A-D**) describes why plants must rely on microorganisms in order to absorb nitrogen?

   ☐ **A** The nitrogen in the atmosphere is too dense.

   ☐ **B** The nitrogen in the atmosphere is too unreactive.

   ☐ **C** Plants only need nitrogen in their roots.

   ☐ **D** The nitrogen in the atmosphere is too far away from the plants' leaves.

   [1]

   [Total 2 marks]

2   **Figure 1** shows a simplified diagram of the nitrogen cycle.

Figure 1

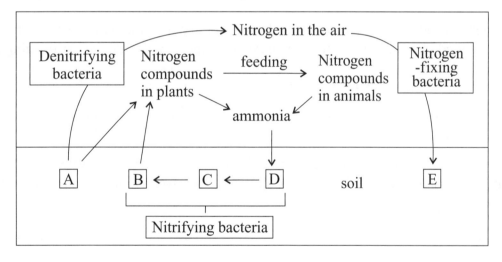

   a) All of the letters on **Figure 1** represent a type of mineral ion.
       List **all** of the letters on **Figure 1** which represent:

   i) nitrites

   ....

   ii) ammonium ions

   ....

   iii) nitrates

   ....

   [5]

Topic 9 — Ecosystems and Material Cycles

b) Lightning can cause a reaction between nitrogen and oxygen in the air to produce nitrates.
   What type of reaction is this?

   ☐ **A** nitrification ☐ **B** denitrification ☐ **C** decomposition ☐ **D** nitrogen fixation

   [1]

c) Describe the role of decomposers in the nitrogen cycle.

   ....

   ....

   [2]

   [Total 8 marks]

3 Yellow leaves are a common symptom of nitrogen deficiency in plants. A gardener noticed that some of his cabbages were showing yellow leaves. He then decided to replant his cabbages in a plot in which he had previously grown pea plants. Peas are a type of legume. After replanting, the cabbages' growth improved and their leaves became less yellow.

(Grade 7-9)

a) Explain why the cabbages' leaves became less yellow after replanting.

   ....

   ....

   ....

   ....

   [3]

b) The gardener decided to use the original cabbage plot to plant other vegetables. Explain why it might be a good idea for him to spread manure or compost on the plot before planting anything.

   ....

   ....

   [1]

c) Denitrifying bacteria are most active in anaerobic conditions, such as in waterlogged soils. Explain **one** reason why the cabbages may show yellow leaves again after a particularly wet season.

   ....

   ....

   ....

   ....

   [3]

   [Total 7 marks]

Exam Practice Tip

The nitrogen cycle is a bit more complicated than either the water cycle or the carbon cycle, and a lot of the names for the different processes sound really quite similar. Before you do anything else, make sure you get the differences between nitrification, nitrogen fixation, decomposition and denitrification sorted in your head. Drawing out the cycle always helps.

Topic 9 — Ecosystems and Material Cycles

Indicator Species

1 Indicator species can be used to assess whether a river is polluted or not. (Grade 4-6)

a) Name **two** species you would expect to find in a highly polluted river.

....

[2]

b) A student finds stonefly in several samples of a river's water.
What does this suggest about the level of pollution in the river? Explain your answer.

....

[2]

[Total 4 marks]

2 Lichens grow on the bark of trees. They are sensitive to the concentration of sulfur dioxide in the air, which is given out in vehicle exhaust gases. A road runs by the side of a forest. Scientists recorded the number of lichen species growing on trees in the area. **Figure 1** shows the results.

Figure 1 (Grade 6-7)

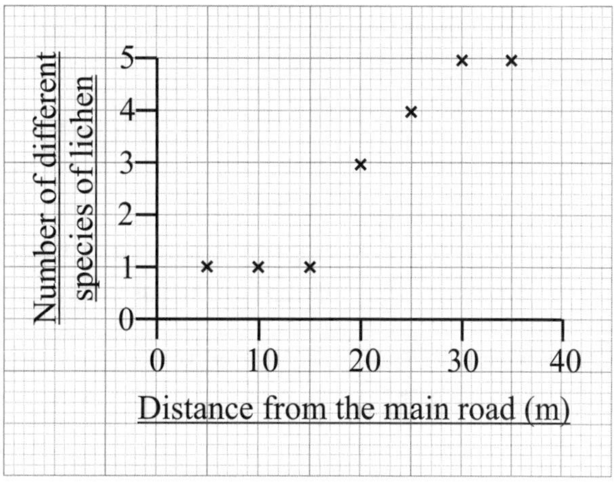

A graph titled Figure 1. The y-axis is labelled "Number of different species of lichen" ranging from 0 to 5. The x-axis is labelled "Distance from the main road (m)" ranging from 0 to 40. Points plotted: (5, 1), (10, 1), (15, 1), (20, 3), (25, 4), (30, 5), (35, 5).

a) Describe the relationship between the number of species of lichen growing on the bark of trees and the distance from the main road. Suggest an explanation for your answer.

....

....

[2]

b) Based on these results, what is the minimum distance a road should be from a forest to allow at least four species of lichen to grow?

....

[1]

c) Give **two** limitations of using indicator species to determine how polluted an area is.

....

....

[2]

[Total 5 marks]

Topic 9 — Ecosystems and Material Cycles

Decomposition

Are the following statements true or false? Circle the correct answers.

Microorganisms carry out decomposition of dead material.	True / False
A greater oxygen availability lets decomposition take place faster.	True / False
A temperature which is too high can reduce the rate of decomposition.	True / False
A temperature which is too low doesn't affect the rate of decomposition.	True / False

1   There are many different ways of preserving food. One is to freeze it. *(Grade 4-6)*
This prevents the microorganisms involved in decay from reproducing.

Give **one** other method of preserving food.
Explain how this method prevents or slows down decay.

....

....

....

[Total 2 marks]

2   Many gardeners keep compost bins to allow organic waste from their garden *(Grade 6-7)*
to decompose, so that they can recycle the nutrients in it back into the ground.

a) **Figure 1** shows a compost bin. Choose **one** feature of this compost bin and
explain how it is designed to increase the rate of decomposition.

Figure 1

....

....

....
[2]

b) It's important that the compost is moist, but not too wet.
State why water is necessary for decomposition.

....

....
[1]

c) As the compost decomposes, it generates heat.
What effect will this have on the rate of decomposition? Explain your answer.

....

....
[2]

[Total 5 marks]

3 A group of students were investigating the effect of temperature on the rate of decay of slices of bread.

Figure 2

Time (days)	Percentage of slice covered in mould (%)
0	0
5	2
10	10
15	22
20	50
25	88

Two slices of bread were moistened with water, then sealed in plastic bags after one hour. One slice was refrigerated and the other was stored at room temperature. The slices were inspected every five days and the percentage cover of mould on each slice was estimated using a grid. **Figure 2** shows the results for the slice of bread stored at room temperature.

The results for the refrigerated slice are plotted in **Figure 3**.

a) Add the results for the slice stored at room temperature to **Figure 3**. Draw a curve of best fit.

[3]

b) Between which two time points was the growth of mould at room temperature the fastest?

....

....
[1]

c) Calculate the mean rate of decay for the slice at room temperature between days 15 and 25 of the experiment.

Figure 3

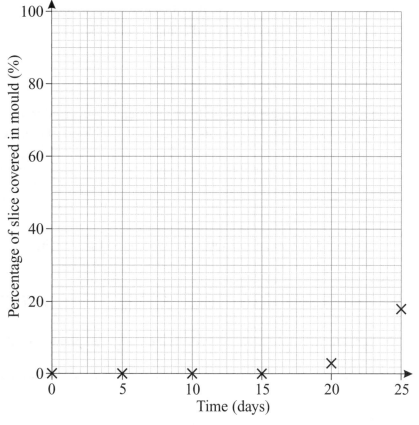

Mean rate of decay = ... % day⁻¹
[2]

d) Use **Figure 3** to calculate the mean rate of decay per hour for the refrigerated slice between days 20 and 25 of the experiment. Give your answer to 2 decimal places.

Mean rate of decay = ... % hour⁻¹
[3]

e) Give **two** variables that should have been controlled in this experiment, in order to make it a fair test.

....

[2]

[Total 11 marks]

Topic 9 — Ecosystems and Material Cycles

Mixed Questions

1 Aerobic respiration transfers energy from glucose. (Grade 4-6)

a) i) Name the subcellular structures where aerobic respiration takes place.

....

[1]

ii) Complete the word equation for aerobic respiration.

glucose + ... → .... + water

[2]

Glucose is obtained through the diet.

b) Once it has passed through the digestive system, glucose is transported around the body in the blood. Name the liquid component of blood.

....

[1]

c) Some of the excess glucose from the diet is converted into glycogen and stored in the liver. Explain what happens to this glycogen if the blood glucose concentration falls below normal.

....

[2]

[Total 6 marks]

2 **Figure 1** shows an example of a woodland food chain. (Grade 4-6)

Figure 1

green plants ⟶ greenflies ⟶ blue tits ⟶ stoats

a) What term would be used to describe the green plants' position in **Figure 1**?

....

[1]

b) The diagram on the right represents a pyramid of biomass for this woodland food chain. Write the name of each organism in the food chain on the correct level of the pyramid.

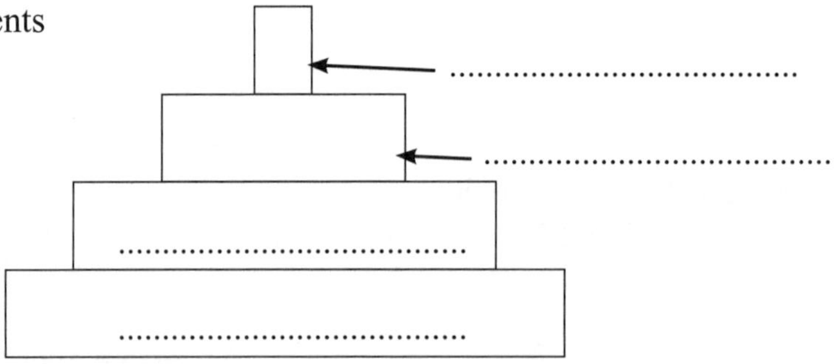

.... ←

.... ←

....

....

[1]

c) Give **one** biotic factor and **one** abiotic factor that may reduce the amount of green plants in this woodland food chain.

Biotic: ....   Abiotic: ....

[2]

[Total 4 marks]

3 Alcohol is metabolised in the liver using alcohol dehydrogenase enzymes. (Grade 4-6)

a) One of the functions of the liver is to break down excess amino acids.

i) Which of the following molecules is made up of amino acids?

☐ **A** a carbohydrate ☐ **B** a protein ☐ **C** a lipid ☐ **D** glycerol

[1]

ii) Name the waste product produced from the breakdown of amino acids, which is excreted by the kidneys.

....

[1]

b) Enzymes:

☐ **A** speed up chemical reactions in living organisms.

☐ **B** are used up in chemical reactions.

☐ **C** are products of digestion.

☐ **D** are the building blocks of all living organisms.

[1]

c) A scientist was investigating the effect of temperature on the rate of activity of alcohol dehydrogenase. **Figure 2** shows a graph of his results.

Figure 2

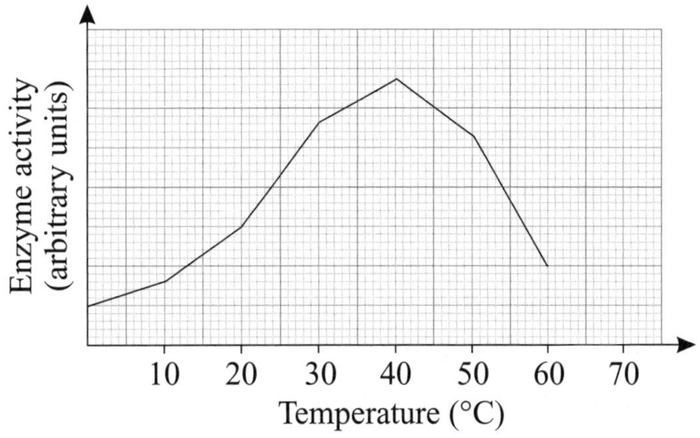

i) What is the optimum temperature for the enzyme?

....

[1]

ii) Suggest and explain the effect a temperature of 70 °C would have on the activity of the enzyme.

....

....

....

[3]

[Total 7 marks]

4 In pea plants, seed shape is controlled by a single gene. **(Grade 6-7)**

The allele for round seed shape is R and the allele for wrinkled seed shape is r.
R is a dominant allele and r is recessive.

a) What is the genotype of a pea plant that is homozygous dominant for seed shape?

....

[1]

b) What is the phenotype of a pea plant that is heterozygous for seed shape?

....

[1]

c) Two pea plants were crossed. All of the offspring produced had the genotype **Rr**.
Construct a Punnett square to find the genotypes of the parent plants.

Genotypes: .... and ....

[2]

[Total 4 marks]

5 A group of scientists are investigating the antibacterial properties of chemicals produced by a species of plant. **(Grade 6-7)**

a) Before they begin their investigation, they need to produce
many individual plants from one parent plant.

i) Describe how they could use tissue culture to achieve this.

....

....

....

....

[3]

ii) Give **one** reason why the scientists may prefer to use tissue culture to produce the plants they
need, rather than allowing them to reproduce naturally.

....

....

[1]

Mixed Questions

b) Once enough plants have been produced, the scientists process them to produce a liquid plant extract. The scientists then test the antibacterial properties of the plant extract by soaking paper discs in different concentrations of the extract and placing them on an agar plate spread with a species of bacteria.

The plates are incubated for two days and the inhibition zones around each disc are then measured. This procedure is repeated three times and the mean results calculated, as shown in **Figure 3**.

Figure 3

Concentration of plant extract	100%	50%	25%	12.5%
Mean radius (mm)	11	8	5	4
Area of inhibition zone (cm²)	3.8	2.0	**Y**	0.5

i) Calculate the value of **Y** to complete **Figure 3**.
   Give your answer in cm² and to 1 decimal place.

   $\pi = 3.14$

   Y = ... cm²

   [3]

ii) Use **Figure 3** to plot a graph of the area of the inhibition zone against the concentration of the plant extract for the 100%, 50% and 12.5% solutions. Draw a line of best fit between the points.

   [3]

iii) Use the graph to estimate the area of the inhibition zone produced by a solution of this plant extract with a concentration of 80%.

....

   [1]

iv) Describe the relationship between the concentration of plant extract and its effectiveness at preventing bacterial growth.

....

   [1]

   [Total 12 marks]

Mixed Questions

6   The menstrual cycle is controlled by hormones. **Figure 4** shows the change in the levels of these hormones during one menstrual cycle. It also shows the change in the lining of the uterus.

Figure 4

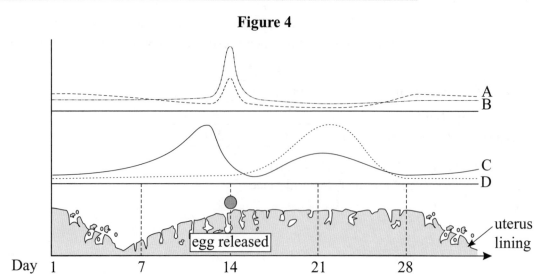

a) Describe how a hormone travels from a gland to its target organ in the body.

....

....

[2]

b) Describe how a high progesterone level affects the secretion of hormones from the pituitary gland.

....

....

[2]

c) i) Which line in **Figure 4** represents oestrogen?

☐ **A**   ☐ **B**   ☐ **C**   ☐ **D**

[1]

ii) Which line in **Figure 4** represents luteinising hormone (LH)?

☐ **A**   ☐ **B**   ☐ **C**   ☐ **D**

[1]

d) Name **two** hormones involved in maintaining the uterus lining.

1. ....

2. ....

[2]

e) State **two** effects of FSH during the menstrual cycle of a woman.

1. ....

2. ....

[2]

[Total 10 marks]

Mixed Questions

7 Crops can be genetically modified so that they produce substances that they wouldn't normally. An example of this is Golden Rice. Read the information about Golden Rice below.

> Golden Rice is a variety of rice that has been genetically modified to produce beta-carotene. Beta-carotene is used in the body to produce vitamin A.
>
> Vitamin A deficiency is a major health problem in some developing countries because many people struggle to get enough beta-carotene and vitamin A in their diet. Golden Rice could be used in these countries to help tackle vitamin A deficiency.
>
> Golden Rice was genetically engineered using a rice plant, a gene from a maize plant and a gene from a soil bacterium.

a) Explain whether vitamin A deficiency is a communicable or non-communicable disease.

....

....

[1]

b) Explain why the genome of Golden Rice will be different to the genome of normal rice.

....

....

[1]

c) Describe the process that may have been used to produce Golden Rice.

....

....

....

....

....

....

....

....

[4]

d) Some people don't agree with the production of Golden Rice in order to tackle vitamin A deficiency. Give **two** potential arguments against its production and use.

1. ....

....

2. ....

....

[2]

[Total 8 marks]

8   A farmer selectively bred her tomato plants so they produced larger fruit. Before she started the selective breeding process she randomly selected eight tomatoes from her original plants (Generation A) and recorded their circumferences. She repeated this on the plants that were produced several generations later (Generation X). Throughout the process she controlled all environmental factors that could affect the growth of her plants. **Figure 5** shows her results.

Figure 5

	Tomato Circumference (cm)								Mean (cm)	Range (cm)
Generation A	9.3	13.8	12.5	10.6	12.7	15.4	14.3	13.0	12.7	6.1
Generation X	18.2	17.4	16.8	15.6	18.1	17.6	17.2	15.9	17.1	2.6

a) i) Explain why the range of the circumferences is smaller in Generation X than in Generation A.

....

....

[2]

ii) Calculate the percentage change in mean tomato circumference between Generation A and Generation X.

.............%

[2]

b) The farmer added fertiliser to the soil that she grew her plants in.
Explain how fertiliser can help a plant to make proteins.

....

....

[2]

[Total 6 marks]

9   Limiting factors affect the rate of photosynthesis.

a) A student was investigating the effect of limiting factors on the rate of photosynthesis by green algae. The student set up two boiling tubes like the one in **Figure 6**.
She also set up a third tube that did not contain any algae.
The colour of the indicator solution changes as follows:

Figure 6

- At atmospheric CO_2 concentration, the indicator is red.
- At low CO_2 concentrations, the indicator is purple.
- At high CO_2 concentrations, the indicator is yellow.

The student covered one of the boiling tubes containing algae with foil. No light was able to reach the algae in this tube. All three tubes were left for several hours at a controlled temperature with a constant light source. The colour of the indicator solution was then recorded. The results are shown in **Figure 7**.

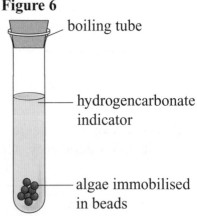

Figure 7

	Algae?	Foil?	Indicator colour at start	Indicator colour at end
Tube 1	yes	yes	red	yellow
Tube 2	yes	no	red	purple
Tube 3	no	no	red	red

i) Name the waste product of photosynthesis.

....
....
[1]

ii) Name the limiting factor of photosynthesis that is being investigated in this experiment.

....
[1]

iii) Explain the results seen in Tube **1** and Tube **2**.

....

....

....

....

....

....
[4]

iv) Give **two** variables that needed to be controlled in this experiment.

1. ....

2. ....
[2]

b) A scientist investigating the effect of limiting factors on photosynthesis sketched the graph shown in **Figure 8**.

Figure 8

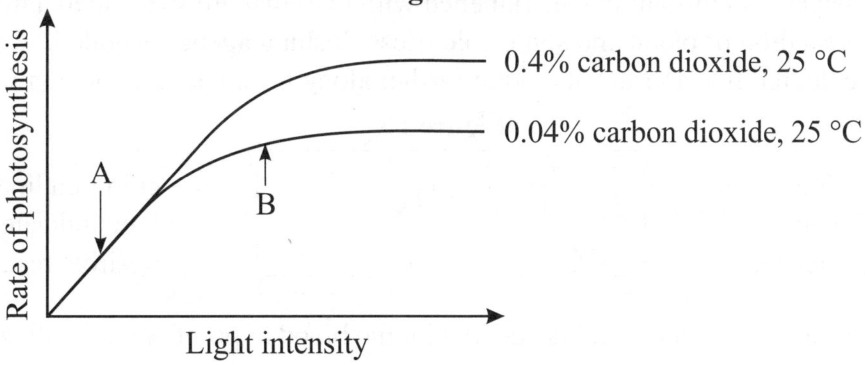

i) Name the limiting factor at point **A**. Explain your answer.

....

....
[2]

ii) Name the limiting factor at point **B**.

....
[1]

[Total 11 marks]

Mixed Questions

10 The life cycle of the protist that causes malaria is shown in **Figure 9**.

Figure 9

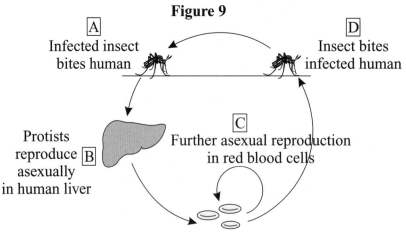

a) Suggest **one** method of blocking the protist's life cycle at point **A**.

....

[1]

b) Name the type of cell division that is occurring at point **B**.

....

[1]

c) Symptoms of malaria include feeling tired and lacking energy. The protist reproduction at point **C** destroys the red blood cells. Explain how this could cause these symptoms of malaria.

....

....

[2]

d) Malaria can be detected in a blood sample using a diagnostic stick, which works in a similar way to a pregnancy test. The stick is made from a strip of paper inside a plastic case. At one end of the stick, the paper contains antibodies (labelled with dye) that are specific to a malaria antigen — this is where a drop of blood and some colourless flushing agent are added. A positive result is revealed if a coloured line appears at a point further along the stick, as shown in **Figure 10**.

Figure 10

drop of blood and flushing agent added here   **A**   **B**   coloured line here indicates a positive result

i) Suggest why some flushing agent is added with the blood at point **A** on the diagnostic stick.

....

[1]

ii) The sample then moves along the stick. Suggest why a coloured line appears at point **B**.

....

....

....

....

[4]

[Total 9 marks]

Mixed Questions

BEQ41